GAIA WARRIORS

URGENT

THE FIGHT IS ON!

Nicola Davies

With an afterword by
James Lovelock

CONTENTS

Section Two
Gaia Warriors

Section Three
Afterword by James Lovelock

Abel & Cole

"Please look after our box, keep it dry, and leave it out for us.
You never know… you might see it again someday.

INTRODUCTION

by NICOLA DAVIES

Most people don't like change. They see it as scary or uncomfortable or both. But if nothing ever changed we'd still be sitting in a cave chewing on old mammoth bones. Ever since the Big Bang our universe has always changed. So we shouldn't be too scared by the fact that the climate of our home planet is changing now, and we will have to change too, if we are to survive.

This book is about **how** and why Earth's climate is changing. But it is also about the **people**, all over the world, who are finding ways for humans to live without hurting our planet. As you read this book you'll be hearing from them: young and old, men and women, scientists, lawyers, business people, architects, designers, mums and dads, kids and campaigners, all sorts of people; people just like you.

We all have a choice. We can carry on as usual and fry. Or we can take the opportunity climate change offers us to make a better world for everyone.

In other words, we can CHOOSE to change for the better.

❝We must be the change we want to see in the world.❞

MAHATMA GANDHI

(Gandhi was an Indian political and spiritual leader in the first half of the 20th century. He lived his ideals of non-violent protest and sustainable living, and had a big impact all round the world.)

Climate Change:
The Basics

" I can't understand why the reaction in the UK to extreme climate change is to turn the newspaper over and start reading an article about the latest tartan-bikini trend. "

CARRI SWANN

(In 2006, when she was 15, Carri was chosen by the Department of Environment, Food and Rural Affairs to be a "Climate Champion" and spread the word about climate change.)

The low-lying Netherlands have always suffered from floods, but rising sea-levels have made people interested in buying floating houses like these.

www.ecoboot.nl

Eagan, Bluepeace

Piles of concrete blocks protect Male, the capital of the Maldives, from storms and rising sea-levels.

UNLESS you've been hiding under a stone for years, you'll have heard about climate change: all those scary predictions about melting ice-caps, killer storms, rising sea-levels and severe droughts. But maybe you've been telling yourself, "Oh, it won't REALLY happen," or "It won't happen for a hundred years."

Well, it's happening right now, **already**, all over the world.

The sea ice in the Arctic has melted to the smallest area ever recorded, and in 2002 an ice shelf in Antarctica the size of Luxembourg broke up and disappeared. The strength of storms, cyclones and hurricanes is increasing, and since the 1960s the number of people whose homes get flooded every year has risen from 7 million to 150 million. Male, the capital city of the Maldives (a country made entirely from tiny islands in the Indian Ocean), has had to build a wall 3.5m high to keep out the rising sea, and the people of Tuvalu – another nation of islands, in the South Pacific – are trying to negotiate settlement rights in New Zealand, ready for when their whole country disappears under the waves. The people of the Netherlands are building floating houses to prepare for the flooding of their low-lying country, while in Western Australia farmers are struggling with declines in rainfall that threaten to put them out of business.

That's just a few of the many thousands of examples of the effects climate change is already having on human lives around the world. In our lifetimes, and the lifetimes of our children and grandchildren, climate change is going to be the biggest challenge human beings have ever had to face.

Yes, it's a real drag that we should be alive at **just** the time when it's all going a bit wrong, and yes, it **is** scary, but sticking our fingers in our ears and going "La la la, it's not happening!" isn't going to help. Neither is going round being gloomy, and telling everyone you meet that "We're doomed, all doomed."

Climate change is happening, but we're not doomed. We can't stop it, but we could slow it down and we could prepare for its effects. It's going to be a big job, and it'll mean changing almost everything about the way we live now – how we light and heat our homes, what transport we use, how we design buildings, how we grow food, how we handle disasters and diseases, even how people and countries work out, together, what's fair and what isn't.

It isn't going to be easy, but it isn't going to be boring, either. In fact, we could all be about to participate in the most exciting period in human history. Never mind "Xbox" and "Wii", "orcs", "Sauron" and "Voldemort"; this is the REAL battle, the battle to save ourselves and our planet from climate catastrophe.

The good news about this battle is that it isn't going to involve guns, blood and killing; the weapons you'll need to help fight it are ideas, energy and determination. The even better news is that there are already lots of people out there fighting, and actually enjoying being part of such an exciting and challenging struggle. Who knows, if you join them, we might just save the world.

" Humans never change unless we have to. And finally, we have to. "

SEVERN CULLIS SUZUKI

(Severn is a young Canadian who has been sticking up for our planet since she spoke to the 1992 UN Earth Summit in Rio de Janeiro when she was 12.)

There are about a trillion books and websites that will tell you all you could ever possibly want to know about climate change (you'll find some of the most useful ones listed at the back of this book). The aim of this section isn't to compete with all these, but to give you a guide to some of the main points. It's in the form of answers to questions that people often ask, especially people who aren't sure that they really believe "the whole global warming thing". So even if you already know all there is to know, you might find these answers useful if you're trying to convince someone that climate change isn't something made up by a worldwide conspiracy of job-seeking scientists and that the greenhouse effect is not a mental illness suffered by gardeners.

" **Global warming – the great big lie. How can they say the Earth is warming up? Just look at our summers – once again this year it is rain, rain, rain and more rain.** "

Contributor to the SUN newspaper online discussion

(someone taking a short-term and short-sighted view of climate change, and getting in a muddle).

WHAT IS CLIMATE CHANGE?

The first thing to understand is that **climate and weather are not the same thing**. As science-fiction writer Robert A. Heinlein once said, "Climate is what you expect, but weather is what you get." But you already know this. You know that a summer picnic is a better bet than a winter one, but that the weather on the day of the picnic could make the summer picnic wet, and the winter one dry (you know this especially well if you live in the UK).

Getting climate and weather muddled up can create confusion: another famous writer, Michael Crichton (who wrote *Jurassic Park* and *Twister*), was doing just that when he wondered how scientists can claim that the climate is changing when they can't get weather forecasts right. Day-to-day weather may be very unpredictable, as we all know, but over years and decades the ups and downs in temperature, wind and rain can be seen to be part of a stable and predictable pattern; that pattern is what we call climate.

Because climate is a pattern that reveals itself only over many years, you can't look at climate in close-up; it has to be the big picture. A single bit of weather – an extra-hot summer month or an unusually fierce storm – tells you as much about climate as the trunk of a single tree tells you about the whole forest. But a STRING of hot summers or a rise in the number and ferocity of storms **over several years** could show that the big picture – the long-term pattern of climate – is shifting, and that climate **is** changing.

That is what's happening to the Earth right now. The long-term records of weather all over the world (see *How Do We Know That Climate Is Changing?*, page 25) show that the pattern isn't the same as it was 100 or even 50 years ago. The Earth is undergoing climate change. Overall, the planet is getting hotter, which is why some people call what's happening "global warming" or "global heating". But the Earth's increasing temperature could affect all sorts of aspects of the climate – rainfall patterns, winds and storms – so I'm going to use the term "climate change". It seems to be the most commonly used label these days anyhow.

The other term you might come across that's used to describe what's happening to our planet is "the greenhouse effect". It's worth understanding this one, because it actually tells you something about what causes climate change/global warming/global heating.

The greenhouse effect isn't a bad thing; without it we'd be like the moon, boiling when the sun's up and colder than a freezer after sunset, with an average temperature of –18°C! But, unlike the moon, we have an atmosphere which stops us getting too hot or too cold. The atmosphere, along with its clouds and dust, reflects some of the sun's light straight back to space, so it never has a chance to heat us. The remaining sunlight makes it to ground level and is absorbed by the Earth's surface, which heats up. Without an atmosphere, all that heat would be lost straight back into space, so the moment the sun went down we'd be freezing cold again. But the atmosphere traps some of the heat, soaks it up and then radiates it out again: some of it goes up and out into space, and some goes down to the Earth's surface.

This balance of keeping heat in and letting heat out is how the atmosphere keeps us comfortably cosy. (This isn't the way a greenhouse works, but the atmosphere and greenhouse glass both keep what's underneath them warm, so the name has stuck.)

The bad news is that the balance of heating and cooling has been upset. The atmosphere today is trapping more heat than it is losing. In other words, we now have a bigger greenhouse effect than we need, and it's making the Earth hotter and changing our climate.

As the Earth's climate gets hotter, deserts could expand.

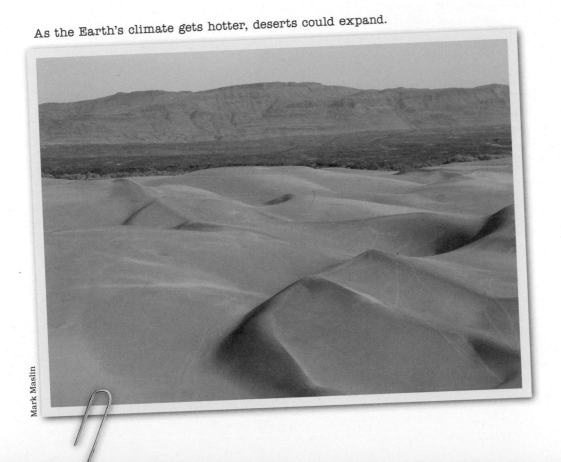

Mark Maslin

Earth-Watching: **Interview**

Dr Don Grainger studies clouds – and smoke, dust and air pollution ... in fact any tiny particle or droplet that floats around in the atmosphere and might affect how much, or how little, of the sun's energy gets reflected back into space. Measuring these floating particles and droplets – known as aerosols – is hard from ground level, so Don and his team from the Department of Atmospheric, Oceanic and Planetary Physics at Oxford University do it from space, using satellites.

Dr D. G. Richards

NASA

"We use two kinds of satellites," Don explains, "geostationary ones that stay in orbit over the same point 35,786km above the Earth's surface, and polar orbit satellites that follow a path like a giant hula hoop, 780km up."

Neither kind can take pictures of the whole Earth at once, but they build a picture up from a series taken as they scan the surface. The pictures get beamed down to Earth, and travel via the internet to Don's computer (next to the two stuffed kiwis in his office). Analysing the pictures – which are taken using both visible light and infrared (heat) – shows not only where the aerosols are, but what they are made of and how much light and heat they

Don exploring in Fiordland, New Zealand.

are reflecting. Don can monitor how the pollution from cities and factories builds up and then disperses, or how the smoke from forest fires mixes with clouds and changes the way they reflect light.

The photographs show the surface of the Earth too, the land and the sea, and the pictures taken using infrared allow Don and his team to monitor the temperature of the surface.

"Sea surface temperatures can be used to understand ocean currents and this could improve our short-term forecasting of climate change."

The pictures show up changes in land use too. Monitoring how much forest gets cut down or how deserts are spreading is very difficult from the ground, but this information can be seen much more clearly on a satellite picture. Don tells me:

"Andy, one of my students, recently showed me new estimates of deforestation rates in the Amazon derived from satellite images."

Here's a photo of Brazilian rainforest taken from a satellite.
The brown areas on the left are deforested.

This matters because forests have a particularly important role to play in climate change (see *Keeping Gaia Green*, page 142).

Although satellite images are used in weather forecasting – we've probably all seen them on the TV weather broadcasts – their value to scientists like Don is in allowing them to look at the bigger picture and monitor the planet in the long term:

"Our expectations of climate change are based on computer models of how the Earth-atmosphere system works," says Don. "Satellite images can be used to help us understand these processes."

A composite image of the aerosol loading in the atmosphere.

Dr A. M. Sayer

AATSR False colour 20080611

An image coloured
to help show cloud
structure.

Dr G. E. Thomas

In other words, what Don's work does is show what the Earth's climate is really doing, not what the computer models expect it to do!

Don and his team would like to understand more about how aerosol pollution is changing the climate, but it will need a new generation of satellite technology to get to grips with the problem properly. In the meantime, there are moments when satellites simply show something wonderful:

"My favourite images are the long parallel lines of clouds caused by the atmosphere bouncing up and down over large mountain ranges."

> **The ice is melting earlier and quicker. I'm worried for my future – the future of my generation.**

LUDY PUDLUK

(An Inuit who has lived in the Arctic all his life, Ludy was a politician before retiring and devoting his time to campaigning for climate change.)

NORTHERN HEMISPHERE

Departures in temperature (°C) from the 1961 to 1990 average

Data from thermometers (red) and from tree rings, corals, ice cores and historical record (blue).

Year

Climate Change 2001: The Scientific Basis. Contribution of Working Group I to the Third Assessment Report of the Intergovernmental Panel on Climate Change. Figure 1. Cambridge University Press.

How Do We Know That Climate Is Changing?

I'm writing this in February in the UK. I'm wearing two pairs of socks, three sweaters and a thick pair of jeans. Meanwhile, my brother in Melbourne, Australia, is probably out in his garden in swimming trunks and a sun-hat. If the temperature can be so different in different parts of the world, how can anyone tell what the whole planet is doing?

The answer is by using **averages**. If you measure the temperature in different parts of the globe – the cold bits, the warm bits, the medium bits – all through the year, then take an average of them all, it gives an average temperature for the whole planet.

This turns out to be about the same as on a coolish day in spring in the UK, around 14°C. Or at least that is what it **used** to be...

People all over the world have been keeping records of temperature for a very long time – in some places for more than 400 years. Long before humans came along with thermometers the planet itself kept a record of its temperature in the patterns of growth in trees and corals and in the ice of glaciers and polar icecaps. Modern climate scientists have taken a very careful look at these records, and, using only the most reliable ones, have put them together with modern temperature measurements to see what the average temperature of the Earth has been doing for the past 1000 years and more. Plotted onto a graph (see opposite) they show there's a bit of up and

The "hockey stick" graph

down in Earth's temperature, year to year, but overall the graph is shaped like a hockey stick. What the now famous "hockey stick" graph shows (even if you aren't a graphs kind of a person) is that since about 1900 the Earth's average temperature has been creeping up, and it is now rising faster than at any time since humans started measuring things ... it's risen 0.5°C since 1970, bringing the average global temperature today to almost 15°C.

Across the world, **snow and ice** are disappearing. In the Arctic, the summer sea-ice cover is 80% less than it was in the 1970s. Glaciers, massive rivers of ancient ice, are melting faster than ever before, in the Arctic, in the Antarctic and on mountain tops around the world; the glaciers that gave Glacier Bay National Park in Alaska its name will almost certainly be gone by 2030.

With so much melting going on, the SEA-LEVEL is rising. This is tricky to measure – what with tides and waves and so on – but scientists agree that since 1900 world sea-levels have gone up by around 20cm and they are now rising faster than ever before.

The warmer the planet, the warmer its oceans get (this adds to sea-level rise too, because water expands as it warms). Warm oceans are what drive tropical storms, and the frequency and ferocity of tropical storms – cyclones and hurricanes – (particularly in the North Atlantic) seems to be increasing.

Temperature doesn't change on its own. It affects wind and rainfall, and there is evidence from across the globe that these are changing too. In Western Australia, rainfall has been dropping for 50 years, and there's now

Angelika Renner (UEA/BAS)

⬆ Ice floes in the Antarctic where in some places the ice is melting faster than ever before.

⬅ As the planet warms, summers could become hotter and drier, making forest fires more frequent.

30% less water in streams and rivers than in the 1970s. Southern Spain is getting drier too, while in northern Europe and North America extreme downpours are more frequent.

If you aren't convinced by human measurements and observations, there is plenty of evidence that animals and plants are already reacting to climate change – much faster than human governments. Most species have a range of temperatures that they prefer to live within, and many of them are having to move to find that comfort zone. In 2003 a huge study of 1,700 different species showed that since 1950 they have moved on average 6km nearer the poles every ten years. Mountain species have moved 6.1m higher every decade. They don't read newspapers or watch TV, but their behaviour is a clear sign that the Earth's climate is changing.

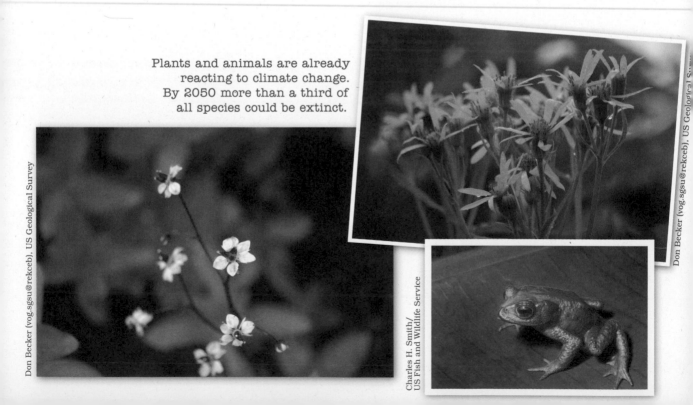

Plants and animals are already reacting to climate change. By 2050 more than a third of all species could be extinct.

Don Becker (vog.sgsu@rekceb), US Geological Survey

Don Becker (vog.sgsu@rekceb), US Geological S

Charles H. Smith/ US Fish and Wildlife Service

Living in a Changed Climate: **Interviews**

Dr Mohamed Ali lives in the Maldives, a country of 1,200 tiny coral islands. He feels the effects of climate change every day:

"We people of the Maldives have relied on our traditional calendar, the Nakaiy system, to predict the seasons, and know when weather will be good for travel, for fishing. But now if I use Nakaiy to plan to travel to outer islands, it doesn't help – the weather turns rough and strange. Unpredictable weather is the main complaint now from farmers and fishermen."

But "strange", unseasonal weather is the least of their problems. Most of the islands are less than 1m above sea-level. With sea-level rising at just under 1cm a year, the Maldives will be gone in a century, and long before that the islands will be uninhabitable. Already people are leaving as the salty ocean taints soil and freshwater supplies, making farming impossible, and storms regularly flood whole islands.

"These islands are so fragile, so vulnerable," says Dr Ali, "but all we can do is protect our local environment – the mangroves and reefs that protect our islands. The rest is beyond our control. We can only ask the international community to cut greenhouse-gas emissions, and allow us to become climate refugees and give us access to land in industrial countries."

The Norwegian Arctic

The Maldives

Greenland's Inuit population

Thomas Debray

Olav Mathis Eira is a reindeer herder. For thousands of years his people, the Sami, have lived by herding the reindeer of the Norwegian Arctic, relying on their knowledge of the Arctic climate and landscape to find good grazing for their animals, even in the deepest winter snows. But the Arctic climate is changing twice as fast as anywhere else on Earth, and that makes finding lichen to eat harder and harder for Olav's animals:

"There are a lot of starving reindeer in some years," he says.

The Sami have moved with the times. They live in modern houses, and have cars and washing machines like other 21st-century Europeans, but their livelihood and their culture depend on reindeer.

"If reindeer herding disappears it will have a devastating effect," says Olav. "Climate change is threatening the entire Sami people."

Reindeer on the hills of Frøyningsfjellet, Norway.

Ice melting in the Arctic is seriously affecting the Inuit way of life.

Mark Maslin

Further north still, Inuit people all around the Arctic are feeling the effects of global warming. **Aqqaluk Lynge**, leader of Greenland's Inuit population, says:

"Climate change is not just a theory to us in the Arctic; it is a stark and dangerous reality."

Like the Sami, the Inuit face the destruction of their way of life and culture:

"Our ecosystem will be transformed, with tragic results," says Aqqaluk. "What will become of the Inuit? Climate change in the Arctic isn't just an environmental issue with unwelcome economic consequences. It's a matter of individual and cultural survival. It's a human issue. The Arctic is our home and homeland." And, Aqqaluk warns, "The serious consequences affecting my people today will affect your people tomorrow."

" **Doesn't global warming cause climate change? There's a link between the two but I'm not too sure what it is.** "

Member of the public, interviewed as part of a UK government report on public understanding of climate change

(Actually this person understands it all rather better than they think they do...)

WHAT'S CAUSING CLIMATE CHANGE?

To answer this question we need to start without the **"change"** and ask, **"What causes climate?"** This is a HUGE question and scientists are still puzzling over the details, but here are the basics. The sun is the most important cause of climate. Without its energy the Earth would be a cold, dead piece of rock. The sun shines on our planet and warms it up. But it doesn't warm it equally. Because the Earth is a sphere, sunlight hits both ends – the North and South poles – at a slant, spreading its energy more thinly there than on the tropics. This helps make the Arctic and Antarctic cold, and the tropics hot. Also, the Earth doesn't stand up straight as it goes round the sun, it's tilted; so for six months the north half gets the most sun and for the other six months the south half does, giving us winter and summer.

This unequal warming has another big climate effect: it gives us winds and ocean currents. Air rises as it gets warm, and cold air rushes in underneath to fill the space – hey presto – wind! A similar thing happens in the oceans, warm water expands, flowing over the surface, while cold water sinks. So, with some parts of the planet getting more warmed up than others, there are risings and sinkings of air and water all the time, stirring the atmosphere and the oceans like giant hands. These stirrings set up planet-wide patterns of winds, which move clouds and rain around the Earth, and a vast global plumbing system of ocean currents, which cool some regions and warm others, helping to give each region its distinctive climate. The UK, for example, has a much warmer climate than it should have, given how far north we are, because of the warming effects of the North Atlantic Drift current that goes past our west coast. The colour of the Earth's surface also has an effect on how much the sun warms any bit of it. Dark bits, or to give them their proper scientific label, "areas with a low ALBEDO", like seas and forests, soak up the sun's warmth. Light bits, areas with a high albedo, especially the bright-white polar ice-caps, bounce the sun's rays straight back to space so they never warm us (try going out on a sunny day with a black T-shirt on, and then a white T-shirt, to see how this works for yourself). The high albedo of the polar ice-caps has a cooling effect on the whole planet.

Oceans and forests – the dark, low-albedo bits – tend to warm us up. But that warmth gives us another important part of our climate – rain, because water evaporates from warm seas and moist forests to form clouds. Clouds can be climate-coolers: they cool whatever they formed from – just as sweat cools your skin as it evaporates – and when they cause rain, they cool whatever they fall on. Clouds have a high albedo, so cloud high up over a forest or an ocean can turn a source of warming into a source of cooling. But clouds can also be climate-warmers, holding heat close to the Earth's surface like a blanket. In fact, the heating and cooling effects of clouds are among the things that climate scientists are struggling to understand.

It's complicated, isn't it? So, for a minute, let's really simplify things and think about climate like a central heating system:

◎ Sun provides heat (like the boiler of a central heating system);

◎ Winds and ocean currents soak up the sun's heat and move it around the planet (like pipes and radiators);

◎ Albedo of ice, snow and some clouds cools us down (like uninsulated doors, windows and roof);

◎ Low clouds stop heat escaping, like the insulation in the attic.

Working together, these bits of the central heating system give us the pattern of climate for the planet – cold poles, hot tropics and everything else somewhere in between. But the factor that controls *how* cold and *how* hot the poles and tropics are, the thermostat for the whole planet's central heating system, is the atmosphere. And the setting of that thermostat depends on the greenhouse effect.

Now, the really important thing to know about the greenhouse effect is that it is created by gases that make up less than 2% of the Earth's atmosphere. The most important of these "greenhouse gases" are water vapour, carbon dioxide (CO_2), and methane. They form a tiny part of the atmosphere, but, like the drop of red paint that turns a tin of white paint pink, these greenhouse gases have a big, big, **BIG** effect; if their concentration rises, even a little, then the atmosphere traps more of the sun's warmth.

And that is just what has happened: CO_2 levels are 30% higher than they were 200 years ago, and methane levels have gone up by a whacking 240%). Water vapour has increased too, because the warmer the Earth becomes, the more water vapour there is in the air. All in all, the Earth's thermostat has been turned up.

We can't see or smell what's happened to the atmosphere all around us – but it's happened all the same, and that little change in the mixture of our air is what is causing climate change.

Air Monitor: **Interview**

Michael Trudeau works for the US Government's National Oceanic and Atmospheric Administration (NOAA) in Colorado. He's one of many scientists all over the world who monitor the chemistry of the atmosphere.

"I spend most of my days in shorts and sandals, sitting at my desk," he says, "imagining how human activities might influence greenhouse gases, and the Earth's climate.

Hawaii   Colorado

Michael Trudeau

Right now, I'm working on a computer model that calculates atmospheric concentration of methane."

Methane is the next most important greenhouse gas after CO_2. It comes from wetlands, rice paddies and the digestive systems of cows and sheep, but also from the burning of forests, the mining of fossil fuels and the landfill sites where we dump our rubbish. Even though there's less of it in the atmosphere than of CO_2, its greenhouse effect is 60 times more potent and there's growing scientific evidence that it could cause big, fast warming. Mike explains:

"Small increases in global temperatures could increase methane emissions from wetlands and release methane from under the sea. An increase in the concentration of such a potent greenhouse gas could produce sudden warming."

NOAA employee Paul Fukumura is monitoring changes in greenhouse gases by taking air samples at the Mauna Loa Observatory in Hawaii.

Mike's computer models of course need accurate information to work on, so Mike measures how much methane is in the atmosphere, with a device that uses a laser beam:

"It works on the principle that methane absorbs certain wavelengths of light," Mike explains. "It's like shining a light through a cup of coffee: the stronger the brew, the less light makes it through the cup."

Scientists are paying a lot of attention to methane right now, because, while CO_2 stays in the atmosphere for 100 years, making any change in CO_2 emissions slow to show an effect, methane stays in the air for just nine years.

"So," Mike says, "if we change the amount we emit, we'll produce a change in the atmosphere on shorter time-scales."

This means that cutting methane emissions – through changes in how we dispose of our rubbish, and how we farm the land – could put a relatively fast-acting brake on global warming.

"But before governments can sit down and draft agreements about emissions," says Mike, "greenhouse-gas inventories for each nation need to be understood."

Mike's work is helping supply that information, about who emits which greenhouse gases and how much.

"The real questions," Mike concludes, "are how bad are we going to let things get through our inaction, and what kind of world do we want to pass on to our children?"

" It's true we've had higher CO_2 levels before. But then, of course, we also had dinosaurs. "

NOAA scientist

(NOAA, the National Oceanic and Atmospheric Administration, researches and monitors everything about the sea and the air in America. It's a very serious scientific organization, which doesn't really do jokes; maybe that's why this scientist, interviewed by author Elizabeth Kolbert for her book "Field Notes from a Catastrophe", didn't give a name.)

But Hasn't Climate Always Changed?

The short answer to this question is "yes". The Earth is seriously ancient – around 4,500 million years old – and in its long life it's been a lot hotter and a lot colder than it is now. In just the last couple of hundred million years – pretty recently as far as the Earth is concerned – its climate has switched from hothouse to ice-house. Around 130 million years ago, when dinosaurs were stomping about the planet, there were no ice-caps and it was warm enough for tropical plants to grow near the poles. But around 50 million years ago the Earth began to cool down, and for about the last 13 million years it's been an "ice house", with two frozen poles and more than twenty ice ages in the last 3 million years, which covered Europe and North America in a layer of ice up to 3km thick.

If the Earth's climate has changed so much naturally in the past, why should we be worried about climate change now? Well, two reasons. The first is that the whole of human civilization – agriculture, cities, art, science, hot baths, iPods and jet planes – has developed in a nice, balmy interglacial (that's the period of time between ice ages), which has given the Earth ten thousand years of easy, stable climate. There have been some variations, warm periods and cold snaps lasting a few hundred years, which are too small to count as major changes to the global climate but can be linked to crop failures, famine, mass migration and even the collapse of entire civilizations. So we know that even quite mild climate change can be pretty destructive.

The second reason is that the more scientists find out about why and how climate changed in the past, the more it confirms that we could be in for a hot future, because of increasing levels of greenhouse gases in our atmosphere today.

That isn't to say that greenhouse gases have been the only thing involved in past climate change; on the time-scale of the Earth's long life, there have been many changes in the planetary central heating system. The positions of the windows, doors, radiators and piping have altered because of continental drift. This is the slow waltzing of the continents, which happens over tens of millions of years. It changes the position of the land, makes seas, blocks or opens the flow of heat-carrying ocean currents, and influences the formation of polar ice-caps which can form only when there is land at, or near, the poles. One of the causes of the shift from dino-hothouse to ice-house was Antarctica breaking away from the other continents, allowing ocean currents to flow all round it and cool it down. Over millions of years, isolated down there at the South Pole, it cooled enough to freeze. Having a giant ice-cube at the bottom of the world cooled the whole planet down.

The heat we get out of the boiler, too, has varied over time. The amount of energy we get from the sun peaks slightly every eleven years with the activity of sunspots (dark spots on the sun's surface) and cycles. It also changes because of regular variations in the Earth's orbit round the sun, which can take tens or even hundreds of thousands of years. Three million years ago, with the top and bottom of the world already in the freezer and the whole planet on the cool side, the "lows" and "highs" of these variations almost certainly helped to turn ice ages on and off.

But this isn't the whole story. Research has shown that every time there has been a climate shift, there has also been a change in the level of greenhouse gases in the atmosphere. Fifty-five million years ago, when the Earth was already in a hothouse phase, there was a sudden spike in levels of greenhouse gases. It's too long ago for us to be able to say which gases and exactly how fast their levels went up, but the likely candidate is methane, released from stores under the sea by the already high temperatures. Straight afterwards, the Earth's temperature shot up by five degrees over about a thousand years – a blink of an eye in Earth history terms.

But soon after that mega heatwave, greenhouse gas levels began falling again, and Earth began to cool – 30 million years before Antarctica had broken away to planet-cooling isolation at the South Pole and not linked to any of the cycles in the sun's input. Greenhouse gases went on falling and Earth went on cooling, so when Antarctica did at last break away, Earth was already on the way to the ice house.

Much more recently, the cycles of ice age and interglacial seemed linked with greenhouse-gas levels, as well as with sun cycles. Since this freeze/thaw pattern began around 3 million years ago, there have been more than twenty ice ages and interglacials. Every time CO_2 and methane levels fell (by about a third or a half), there was an ice age, and every time they rose again, there was an interglacial.

The big question is, of course, did changes in CO_2 and other greenhouse-gas levels **cause** global temperatures to change? It's hard to be absolutely sure about the sudden temperature change of 55 million years ago – although it seems very likely. The evidence from the ice ages is much clearer. It shows that CO_2 levels rose AND THEN temperatures rose. It isn't a precise recipe – so many spoonfuls of CO_2 gives so many degrees of rising temperature – and it's obvious that other factors have been involved too, but it's pretty clear that greenhouse gases, and CO_2 in particular, have played a major role in driving climate change and controlling the Earth's thermostat.

We now have the highest levels of greenhouse gases in the atmosphere for 800,000 years. If those levels of greenhouse gases go on rising at their current rate, by 2050 they'll be higher than they've been for several million years. And from all we know of what's happened in the past, that will mean a much hotter future.

Measuring the Climate of the Past: **Interview**

Nerilie Abram is a paleoclimatologist – someone who studies what climate was like in the past – and she's been busy drilling holes in the Antarctic, to get long cylinders of ice – called cores – tens of thousands of years old.

Paleoclimatologists like Nerilie are detectives, using clues of all sorts to build a picture of what climate used to be like: the fossils of plants and animals; the shells of plankton and grains of pollen in mud at the bottom of lakes and seas; tree rings; layers in rock; radioactive materials – all these provide pieces of the picture. But for Nerilie, ice cores are the tops:

The Antarctic

Nerilie exploring a crevasse in the ice near the British Antarctic Survey base at Rothera.

"Ice cores let you put together all the different parts of the puzzle," she says. "There's no other kind of record that can tell you so much about so many different parts of the climate system."

The amount of salt in the cores shows how hard the wind was blowing off the sea, so researchers can reconstruct how stormy the climate was; volcanic dust in the cores shows when volcanoes erupted; and bands in the ice show where it melted and thawed again as the temperature rose and fell. Ice can even tell researchers what the temperature was like elsewhere on the planet when the ice was formed. Nerilie explains:

"Heavier isotopes (forms) of water take more energy to lift out of the ocean and blow to the Antarctic to make snow. So when the climate is warmer, there are more heavy isotopes in the snow falling on Antarctica. It's a chemical signal of climate, locked in as the snow turns to ice."

Perhaps best of all, ice cores contain little bubbles of ancient air:

Ice-core drilling camp on top of James Ross Island which was home to seven scientists for two months.

Nerilie Abram

"These are the only direct way we have of knowing exactly what the composition of the atmosphere was in the past – including greenhouse-gas concentrations."

Nerilie and the team from the British Antarctic Survey in Cambridge, UK, were drilling on the mountainous James Ross Island, a part of the Antarctic Peninsula. The ice there is 360 metres thick, and around 25,000 years old at the bottom. They drilled "cores" in sequence from the surface – "now" – to the bottom – "25,000 years ago",

Nerilie Abram

The barrel of the ice-core drill with an ice sample inside.

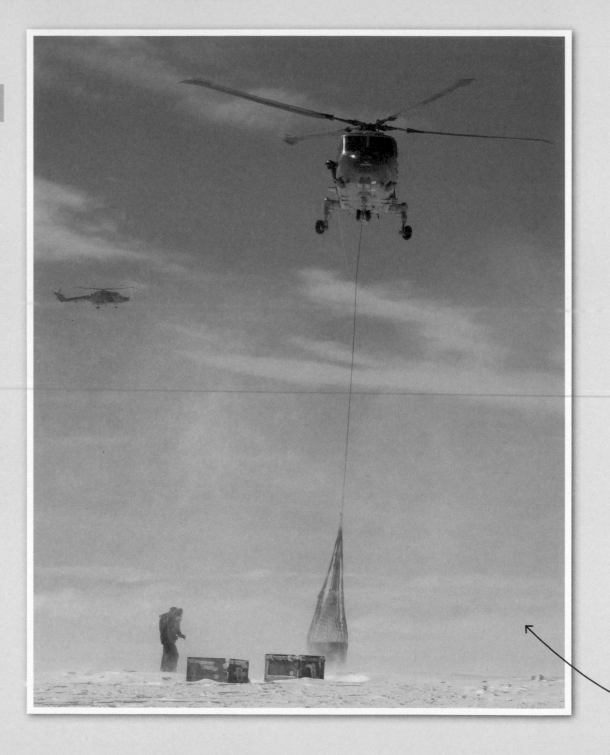

then packed them onto a refrigerated ship to be taken back to Cambridge.

Nerilie's latest ice cores are in the lab now, and she hopes they are going to provide answers to some important questions:

"The Antarctic Peninsula, where we were working, is warming faster than the rest of Antarctica. Our ice cores will tell us whether this has happened before and how it's related to temperature change. They'll help us to work out how fast the Antarctic ice sheets might melt in future, and how fast sea-levels might rise."

Nerilie may spend her days looking at an ancient ice-cube, but she definitely has her mind on the future:

"Scientists are no longer trying to convince people that global warming is happening," she says. "We're trying to work out what it will be like, how to plan for it and how to prevent the worst-case scenario."

Everything for the ice-core drilling camp was brought to the site by two Lynx helicopters operating off the Royal Navy ship HMS *Endurance*. At the end of the project everything was removed again, so that the site was left in a pristine condition.

" **A changing environment will affect Alaska more than any other state, because of our location. I'm not one, though, who would attribute it to being man-made.** "

SARAH PALIN
Republican Party vice-presidential
candidate in 2008

(This quote, from an interview she did
in August 2008, shows the depth of her
understanding of climate-change issues!)

Is Climate Change Our Fault?

We know that our climate is changing, and we can be pretty sure it's because levels of greenhouse gases, CO_2 in particular, have risen. But we also know that levels of greenhouse gases went up and down like a monkey on a ladder long before humans were around to influence them. How do we know that this time it's our fault?

One way is to take a good look at the natural sources of greenhouse gases in our atmosphere. Unlike continental drift or changes in the sun's energy, the atmosphere – the Earth's thermostat – is actually controlled by life itself. The vast web of living things – microbes, plants and animals – interacts with sea, air and rock to form a single interdependent system, and behaves as if it were one giant body. This mega system was given the name **Gaia** by James Lovelock more than 30 years ago. Gaia was a pretty wacky idea back then, but now most scientists accept that it is a useful way to think about how our planet works. It's also much quicker to write than "vast web of living things interacting with...".

Gaia creates our atmosphere and is constantly soaking up and releasing greenhouse gases. For example, every time you or any other animal on the planet breathes out (respiration), CO_2 is put into the air, but every time a plant grows, it takes some CO_2 out of the air and uses it (photosynthesis). On a longer time-scale, the oceans, rocks and soil take CO_2 out of the air too:

it dissolves in oceans, and tiny plants and animals take up some of it and make their shells with it; when they die, their shells sink to the sea-bed and the CO_2 they contain is locked away for thousands, or even millions, of years. Rocks and soil take CO_2 out of the air by reacting with it and turning it into a different chemical – a process called weathering, which is speeded up by plants and microbes on the surface of rocks and in the soil. And there are similar toings and froings for methane and water vapour.

Scientists have added up all these natural sources of greenhouse gases, now and in the past, and fed them into a computer model to see if they create the changes in climate that we're experiencing in the real world (see *If It's Only a Few Degrees, What Difference Will It Make?*, page 61). What they've found is that the natural sources of CO_2 and other greenhouse gases add up nicely to account for the real ups and downs in global temperature in the PAST, but they don't match the temperatures that have been measured for the last 50–100 years. Only when the scientists add in the CO_2 and greenhouse gases from **our** activities – our coal- and oil- and gas-burning, from all our cars and factories, power stations and farms – do the sums add up. The only way to explain why there is so much greenhouse gas in the atmosphere is that it's because of **us**.

Normally, Gaia balances the processes that put CO_2 and other greenhouse gases into the atmosphere with the processes that take them out. This balancing act isn't perfect and it doesn't work very fast, but over the billions of years of the Earth's history it's been a pretty robust system. It works through a series of what's called negative-feedback systems. For example, if

CO_2 levels rise, then so does temperature; plant growth and weathering are boosted, and so CO_2 levels drop again and temperature follows. This is part of the trigger for ice ages and interglacials, and it is the system that returned greenhouse gases to a more normal level after that massive spike 55 million years ago.

Mostly Gaia keeps greenhouse gases, and therefore the thermostat setting, at about the same level for tens of thousands of years at a time. But if the feedback systems are hugely overloaded in either direction, the thermostat can change to a different setting. For example, at the start of the dino-hothouse period, huge amounts of volcanic activity over hundreds of thousands of years loaded the atmosphere with so much greenhouse gas that the thermostat switched to "hotter". After the dino-hothouse period, weathering of the rocks of the newly-formed Himalayas caused such a large, long-term fall in CO_2 levels that the Earth's thermostat turned to "cooler".

There's plenty of evidence to show that some of Gaia's negative feedbacks are under severe pressure. For example, rising sea temperatures are slowing the growth of marine plants; this is a double whammy because not only does it reduce the amount of CO_2 they soak up, but also it reduces the formation of nice cooling clouds, which algae help to form by pumping cloud-seeding droplets of chemicals into the air. So seas get warmer and these effects get worse. Cutting down tropical forests is another case of our knocking a hole in a useful feedback system and seriously shooting ourselves in the foot (we're destroying about 50 football pitches worth every day). Dead trees release all the CO_2 they collected in their lifetime and, of course, can't grow and

NOAA News Photo/FEMA

Volcanic eruptions have had a big effect on Earth's climate in the past
but have little to do with global warming that is happening now.

soak up any more CO_2. That CO_2 stays in the atmosphere, again driving

the temperature up, and causing droughts which threaten remaining forests,

and so on.

There's no volcanic eruption we can blame for our current greenhouse-gas

levels, and there are no emerging Himalayan mountains to soak them up, so

we can't say this situation is Gaia's fault and we can't hope she'll get us out of

it. We have overloaded our atmosphere with greenhouse gases, damaged the

living systems that might help take them out again and turned our planet's

thermostat to "hotter". Not very bright, is it?

Who's the Climate-Change Baddie?

Deciding who's the biggest CO_2 baddie isn't easy. CO_2 hangs around for about a century and so gets pretty well mixed into the whole atmosphere. So any particular country's CO_2 doesn't just sit like a guilty cloud over the top of it, ready to be measured; the amount of it has to be calculated from how much fossil fuel has been used. Also, as CO_2 lasts so long, it isn't just who's pumping out the CO_2 now who's caused climate change, it's who was doing it 50 years ago. And whose CO_2 emission is it, if one country's industry creates emissions while making stuff for another country to use? (Just think of all the things we buy in the UK that say "Made in China".) Overall we know that about four-fifths of the extra CO_2 in the atmosphere comes from our industrial way of life, but the other fifth is the result of deforestation (see *Keeping Gaia Green*, page 142), so some countries that don't burn much fossil fuel could turn out to be top CO_2 baddies if we looked at their record of cutting forests down – Brazil and Indonesia, for instance.

This jungle has been burned down so that crops can be planted instead.

Jami Dwyer

A LINE-UP OF THE WORST OFFENDERS

	70kg
	60kg
	50kg
	40kg
	30kg
	20kg
	10kg
	0kg

America   Britain   China   Bangladesh

Daily greenhouse-gas emissions for each American are the equivalent of
67 kg CO_2, as much as for six Chinese, two Britons and twenty-seven Bangladeshis.

WORLDWIDE CO$_2$ EMISSIONS PER PERSON

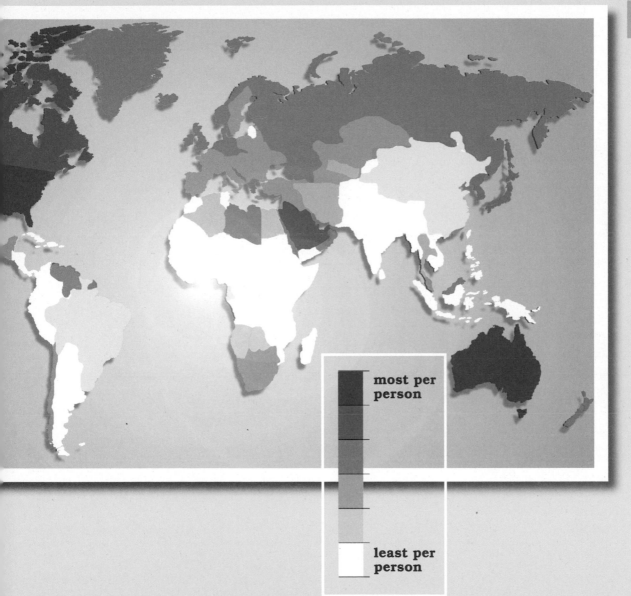

most per person

least per person

" We are going to see a world in which calamities – famines, great loss of life, big storms – are much more common...

Global warming is the biggest problem facing us this century, bigger even than the problems of global terrorism. "

LORD OXBOROUGH
(i.e. BIG, BIG Boss)
Chief Executive Officer, Shell

(yes, that's
Shell,
the oil
company)

If It's Only a Few Degrees, What Difference Will It Make?

From what we can tell about past climate change, a few degrees is all it takes to make a big difference. The Earth four degrees colder than we are now was in the grip of an ice age, while when it was just five degrees warmer, on average, than we are, it was a dino-hothouse with palm trees at the poles. Less than one degree's worth of cooling 700 years ago brought on the "Little Ice Age", with crop failure, famine and plague across Europe. We know that, right now, the not-quite-one-degree rise in average global temperatures is already having a big impact on the world – shrinking ice-caps and glaciers, raising sea-levels, and causing floods, droughts and shifts in the distribution of plants and animals.

One reason that even a small rise in average temperatures can have a big impact is that it can mean changes in **highest** temperatures. The heat wave that hit Europe in the summer of 2003, for example, broke highest-temperature records in four countries and killed 50,000 people. In 1998 and 2002 the water temperature in the Pacific and Indian oceans also broke records, rising high enough to damage and even kill coral reefs. Although it's impossible to tie one specific weather event to global warming, the frequency of these extreme temperatures is increasing.

Another reason is that some places are warming faster than others.

Temperatures in the Arctic have risen twice as much as on the rest of the planet. This is why Arctic ice is disappearing, and the frozen-hard soils of the Arctic – the permafrost – are turning soggy, causing trees, houses, lakes and roads to sink into the mud. Parts of Antarctica are also warming up faster than the average: the temperature of the Antarctic Peninsula is rising by half a degree every ten years, so it's not so surprising that a Luxembourg-sized bit of the Antarctic ice shelf broke up in 2002.

Polar regions are particularly sensitive to temperature change because it takes only a small rise in temperature to go from "freeze" to "thaw", and if our poles thaw, they won't be able to do the planet-cooling job that they do now, so Earth will get hotter still. This is the key to another reason relatively small changes in temperature can pack a big punch: they can trigger positive-feedback loops that speed up warming and make climate change worse. For example, melting ice-caps mean a smaller area of bright white on the Earth's surface, so albedo goes down, and there are more dark areas to soak up more of the sun's warmth, causing further rises in temperature and even more melting of the ice-caps.

The hotter Earth gets, the more of these nasty loops we could get caught in.

Of course, the not-quite-one-degree rise in global temperatures that has already happened isn't the end of our current climate change. Even if we stopped putting any more greenhouse gases into the air, the temperature would still go on rising, because the CO_2 we've already put into the atmosphere will hang around for almost a hundred years. Right now, human activities are putting CO_2 and other greenhouse gases into the atmosphere faster than ever before, so we'll get warmer still.

One way to work out how much hotter it might get and what that might mean for the Earth's climate is to make a computer model of how things could pan out. Computer models of climate change include absolutely everything that science knows about climate and how it works: measurements of temperature, rain, wind, and ocean currents; the impact of forests, deserts and volcanoes; the variations in the energy input from the sun; the amount of greenhouse gases in the atmosphere; even the effect of vapour trails from aircraft and pollution from cars and factories. Facts and figures are combined with the best information we have about how all these components fit together, and all of it is added to the computer mix. Then the models are run like a fantastically complicated computer game to show how climate might play out under different sets of conditions. The accuracy of models is checked by "hindcasting" – using a model to show how climate changed in the past; if a model re-creates a climate very close to what things were really like, then it can be used to predict what might happen in the future.

These are the sorts of models that the Intergovernmental Panel on Climate Change (IPCC – see *Glossary*, page 188) has used to try to predict how climate is going to change. What the panel has come up with is that over the next 90 years or so, the Earth is going to warm up by 1.5–4.5°C. It's not that the models can't give a more accurate prediction of warming, it's just that different sets of information fed into the models give different answers. If, for example, we cut emissions of greenhouse gases, then the 1.5°C end of the range is more likely; if we go on increasing our emissions, as we are now, then we'll wind up at the top end of the range; and if we do nothing either way, we'll be in the middle – an increase of about three or four degrees.

This sounds pretty modest, until you look at the last time the Earth was three degrees hotter. That was three million years ago, and back then there was far less ice at the poles and the seas were 25m deeper than they are now. A world three degrees hotter would be very different from the world we are used to. The best climate models predict droughts, floods and rising sea-levels. This will mean water shortages, crop failures and famine, plus the spread of diseases like malaria: by 2080, 600 million more people could be facing starvation and 320 million more could suffer from malaria. Coastal cities like London and low-lying countries like the Netherlands could suffer frequent floods and start to drown in the rising seas. None of the predictions made by climate models about the three-degree-hotter world says "All OK, just a bit warmer in the summer!". In fact one possibility for Britain is a climate with cooler, wetter summers and colder winters, because melt-water from the Arctic glaciers could cause the seas around us to be colder.

A rise of more than three degrees takes us into the territory of nasty feedback loops that could accelerate climate change and make things even hotter.

Another danger sign is that computer models tend to assume that climate change happens in a nice smooth way, a bit more every year, when in reality climate can change in fits and starts, so we could be in for some sudden shocks. What's more, some parts of the system are changing much faster than the models predicted – Arctic ice, for example, is disappearing more quickly than the models indicated it might.

And one more thing to remember: at the moment greenhouse-gas emissions aren't going down or even staying the same; they are rising faster than ever before.

All in all, it's not looking good. But we do still have time to improve our prospects. The computer models show that the biggest temperature rises are likely **if we don't do anything about cutting the amount of greenhouse gases we put into the atmosphere**. Which means if we DO cut our emissions, we have a chance of keeping the temperature rises smaller. We can't stop climate change happening, but we CAN slow it down, try to keep ourselves out of some of the most horrible feedback loops and buy ourselves a bit more time to adapt to the problems it will present.

It won't be a picnic. There will be further rises in sea-levels, more damaging storms, less predictable rain for our crops, fierce heat waves and possibly some nasty climate surprises that we can't foresee. But if we cut our emissions we stand a chance of keeping civilization together and holding on to some of our most important ecosystems, like the Amazon rainforest.

If we don't, we risk taking all the fun there is right out of the world.

Nasty Shocks and Tipping Points:
Interview

"Think about what happens when you lean back in a chair," says **Tim Lenton**, Professor in Earth System Science at the University of East Anglia, in the UK. "You get to a certain point where a small nudge will send you falling backwards onto the floor. That is the tipping point, the boundary between one stable state – sitting up – and another – sprawled on the floor."

Tee Rogers-Hayden (UEA)

Toppling chairs may seem pretty far removed from climate change, but Tim and scientific colleagues from around the world think that parts of the Earth's climate system could have tipping points just like a tilted chair:

Tim up a mountain, on a research trip in South Island, New Zealand.

"Nudge the system past a certain point," Tim says, "and a big change will start to occur."

The things that Tim and his colleagues have identified as being vulnerable to this kind of change include ice sheets in Greenland and the Western Antarctic, the Atlantic thermohaline circulation (what's commonly referred to as the Gulf Stream – see *Glossary*, page 189), the Indian summer monsoon and the Amazon rainforest. What this means is that if climate warms to even a little above the tipping point for these places, they could switch from one state to another – from frozen to melted, from rain to drought, from flowing to not flowing, from forest to grassland. And just as with a tipping chair, once they start to happen these changes are irreversible.

What's more, passing one tipping point could trigger others, like a row of dominoes. For example, if the tipping point for melting of the Greenland ice shelf was passed, the melt-water would stop the Atlantic thermohaline circulation; this in turn would keep warmer water in the Southern Ocean and speed up the melting of the West Antarctic ice sheet.

Courtesy of the US Geological Society

Sea ice on the Arctic Ocean

It's pretty important to know where these tipping points lie, so we can make sure we don't allow the planet to warm up enough to go past them. Tim's research shows that on the approach to a tipping point, the thing that's about to tip behaves oddly – it changes in unusual ways; but spotting this requires very detailed information about the thing – monsoon rains or ice sheet or ocean current – that could be about to tip, and, says Tim:

"Unfortunately, we don't have a good record for many of the most vulnerable parts of the Earth."

We could even have passed some tipping points already:

"We may have passed a tipping point for the Arctic sea ice," Tim says. "Soon it will reach a state where nearly all of it melts every summer. Arctic summers will be warmer, and the atmosphere's circulation patterns will change, so that the climate in northern Europe and North America will be affected."

Although spotting tipping points is hard, so far Tim's research suggests that we are two, three or four degrees away from many of the nasty ones – but that isn't a reason to relax:

"So far," he says, "there's been a lot of talk and very little action. It really needs a combination of individual action and bold global leadership to slow down climate change."

And it isn't a reason for Tim to be gloomy about his job either:

"I have the best job in the world. I try to understand how planet Earth works as whole system."

" Who will have the courage in twenty-five years' time to tell their children, 'Yes, we could have solved this problem, but it was too expensive'? "

HERMAN SCHEER
German Social Democrat MP and president of the
European Association for Renewable Energy

(a man who sees the change to
"greener" technologies as an economic
opportunity, not a burden).

WHAT IF THE SCIENTISTS HAVE GOT IT WRONG, AND WE WASTE MONEY PREPARING FOR SOMETHING THAT NEVER HAPPENS?

In 2007 the IPCC stated in its fourth report, "Human-induced warming of the climate is widespread."

In other words, the collective opinion of the world's most knowledgeable scientists is that there's no longer any doubt about the reality of global warming. So I nearly didn't include this question, because there are very few people left in the world who still believe that climate change just isn't happening. But for the sake of that tiny percentage of brainless human ostriches, I thought it deserved a place in this book.

There are two answers to this question and they are both pretty short. The first is that the money wouldn't be wasted. Reducing our greenhouse-gas emissions to slow climate change means we'd be investing in fuel efficiency and more environmentally friendly ways of doing things. With fossil fuels – oil, coal and gas – not to mention most other natural resources slowly but surely running out, and rapidly rising in price, this makes sound economic sense. Preparing for the impact of climate change we can't avoid, such as the effects of droughts, floods and rising sea-levels, will reduce the suffering of the world's poorest people, who are being hit by these problems right now.

Climate change is already happening, so waiting to see if more predictions come true before we take action is like staring into the glare of the headlights to see if the car will hit you. The longer we wait, the more expensive it's going to be to fix and the more unpleasant it will be to live through. The Stern Review, a big UK government report about how much climate change could cost the whole world, estimated that acting now to limit it would cost about 1% of the world's money every year. *Not* acting now, and having to cope with the worst effects later, could, in the worst-case scenario, end up costing 20% of the world's money every year.

Businesses all over the world are already working hard to cut their CO_2 and other greenhouse-gas emissions **because it saves them lots of money**. Insurance companies, who since 2004 have had to double the amount of money they pay out for damage caused by "natural" disasters, also know that money spent on combating climate change is well spent. They are calling on companies and governments to cut greenhouse-gas emissions and prepare for climate change now, so that floods, storms and hurricanes don't eat all their profits in the future. (Though beware of companies who claim to be "green" or "sustainable" just to sell you something. Look at this to get the idea:

www.planestupid.com/?q=content/you-cant-spell-greenwashing-without-green.)

The second answer is much shorter, and it's this:

What if the scientists have got it right, and we don't do anything?

Think about it. A world getting hotter and hotter; famine, floods and chaos because nobody has prepared for climate change or tried to slow it down.

It's not a gamble any **SANE** person would take.

Columns and Rows

Surfing the net I found a brilliant little You Tube film that explained the arguments about climate change and what we should do about it very simply in a table with two columns and two rows. You can follow this link **www.youtube.com/watch?v=zORv8wwiadQ&feature=channel** to look at it, but in case you can't be bothered, here is my summary:

CLIMATE CHANGE	WE DO EVERYTHING WE CAN TO STOP IT	WE DO NOTHING TO STOP IT
DOESN'T HAPPEN & isn't a big deal	Oops, that means we wasted some money, so... -1	Well, that's no change, so... 0
DOES HAPPEN & is a big deal	Lots of money and effort spent, but we save the world (that'd be a big plus from me) but to keep sceptics happy... 0	Famine, chaos, disaster, how do you score that...? -3
	$= -1$ (So that's money & effort spent needlessly)	$= -3$ (End of civilization as we know it!)

So we need to stop arguing about the rows and make sure we get the right column.

" I am nine years old and even I know that global warming is very bad and dangerous to my future. If we can't stop polluting the air we will all die. "

from NEW SCIENTIST magazine's
website comments board

" The global-warming scenario is pretty grim. I'm not sure I like the idea of polar bears under a palm tree. "

LENNY HENRY
comedian

If nine-year-olds and comedians are worried, maybe we all should be?

It's All Too Big and Scary and There's Nothing I Can Do about It!

It *is* all big and scary, but I don't believe it's the big scariness that makes people feel there's nothing they can do. Humans have a good track record of tackling big scary things, after all – just think of landing on the moon. No, I think the root of "...and there's nothing I can do about it..." lies in the fact that climate change is so hard to get your head around. I mean, how can we little humans, down here, have an effect on something as vastly huge as the whole atmosphere, up there? And how can there be billions of tonnes of anything in the air, when air doesn't seem to weigh anything? You just can't picture it, can you?

So let's try and get some pictures in our heads that will help make climate change seem real enough to do something about. First, that "vastly huge" atmosphere. Instead of looking at it from down here, like shrimps looking up from the bottom of a rock pool, let's look at the Earth from space, the way

Here is what our beautiful planet looks like from space.

NASA

the first moon-walkers did forty years ago. From the moon, the Earth looks small enough to hold in your hand, a beautiful blue and white globe floating in the dead blackness. The atmosphere isn't vast and huge now, in fact it's barely visible, just a wisp of blue, as thin as a wrapping of cling-film. Look at the atmosphere like that, as a see-through veil that's almost not there at all, and it's easier to understand how fragile it is and how it might be damaged by what humans do.

Now, go back down to Earth and stretch out your arms. Imagine a column of air with its base resting on your outstretched arms, going up and up so that its top is seventy miles above you, where air turns into space. Move your arms up and down to jiggle your column about a bit. It doesn't seem to weigh anything because it is pressing on you equally in all directions, even from inside every cell in your body. But it *does* weigh something – quite a lot, in fact: about 10 tonnes! Which is just a little bit less than the weight of CO_2 and other greenhouse gases that you – and all you do, eat and buy – put into the atmosphere every year: 11.6 tonnes.

So, now you can make a mental picture of the greenhouse gas that's getting into the atmosphere every year because of you. (If you live in America you need to imagine a bigger column – one resting on the family dinner table, perhaps, and weighing 25.9 tonnes.)

OK so far? Now scale it up, and imagine everybody in your family, then your school, then your town, each with their own column of greenhouse gases above them. Tonnes and tonnes and tonnes of it, all going into that fragile, wispy atmosphere.

The great thing is that you can do something to protect the atmosphere from all that CO_2, because you have control over your column and you can start to take action right now, action that will make it smaller:

◉ turn down the heater in your room and wear another sweater instead;

◉ turn off the air-conditioning and open a window instead;

◉ take the TV off standby and turn it right off.

Already your column has shrunk. And you can shrink other columns, too – just tell people about their column and how they can shrink it. Tell your government that you'd like them to help everyone with column-shrinking. You have a lot more power than you think.

Yes, whole countries will have to make huge cuts in the amount of greenhouse gases they put into the atmosphere; yes, oceans and forests will have to be protected so that Gaia's natural climate-balancing system is restored; and yes, it will be tens or hundreds of years before our atmosphere has completely recovered. But all that huge change starts with everyone taking responsibility for their own personal column of greenhouse gas. Big? Yes. Scary? Maybe. But let's do it anyway.

Making Sense of Carbon: **Interview**

"If carbon dioxide was purple," says **Antony Turner**, "the sky would now be a different colour. But CO$_2$ is invisible and because we haven't seen it, we haven't paid it enough attention."

Having spent half his career working as a businessman in engineering companies, Antony is now devoting all his time to making sure we all start paying attention to CO$_2$.

His company, CarbonSense, helps businesses and individual people to see the reality of their carbon footprint.

Antony Turner

A kilo of CO$_2$ would fit in a balloon like this 1m across.

"A carbon footprint is the term for all the emissions of CO$_2$ that a person or a company is responsible for," Antony explains.

For people like you and me, that means adding up all the emissions from the electricity we use, the food we eat and the miles we travel. There are lots of websites that help individuals and families work out their carbon footprint (try **campaigns.direct.gov.uk/actonCO2/** or **www.thecarbonaccount.com**). But for whole companies, with hundreds or thousands of factories, offices, vehicles or shops, it's much more complicated. Antony's team of experts looks at every bit of what a business does and adds up the emissions from every part – from making things to advertising them and transporting them to shops; everything, in fact, from the machines in the factory to the fluffy carpet in the director's office!

"We look at the total carbon footprint of any product or service."

That might mean the footprint made by the supplying of several million people with phone and internet services, or the footprint made by the manufacture of a packet of crisps.

Antony's job doesn't end with producing a list of sums:

"The numbers alone are not enough," Antony says, so CarbonSense uses all sorts of techniques, such as specially-created graphics and animations, to help people to visualize the greenhouse-gas emissions of their business and make climate change real for them.

CarbonSense has worked with all sorts of businesses, from TNT – which delivers letters and parcels in 200 countries – to the Honda racing-car team. And every time, really seeing their carbon footprint and understanding what it means makes a difference: companies shift to energy-saving ways of working and start to think seriously about how they can cut their emissions to almost nothing in future.

"If we reach their hearts," Antony says, **"they may**

decide to do something really creative, really out of the box. That's what we hope for."

Of course it isn't just big business that needs to visualize its carbon footprint; we ALL need to do it:

"Every person, organization, community and country needs to know the basic carbon maths, how much they are responsible for and what parts of their lives are the highest-emitting."

Antony calls this being "carbon literate".

"The most important task facing human society now is getting about 1 billion people carbon literate in the next five years," he says. "Human creativity needs to be unleashed for this most massive challenge."

Section Two
Gaia Warriors

66 **There is still time to avoid the worst impacts of climate change, if we take strong action now.** 99

NICHOLAS STERN

(a top, top economist — and a Lord — who has advised governments and banks in the UK and around the world. He's the author of the Stern Review, a UK government report published in 2006, about what climate change is going to cost the world.)

SO, HERE'S THE PROBLEM:

Our planet is warming up. In your lifetime and that of your children it's going to get a lot warmer.

The level of CO_2 in the atmosphere today is 380ppm (that means parts per million; in other words, in every million parts of air, 380 of them are CO_2). Add in the other greenhouse gases, and that gives the same effect as 440ppm of CO_2...

This amount of greenhouse gas in the atmosphere is likely to make the climate at least two degrees warmer than it is now, perhaps even four degrees warmer.

A planet four degrees warmer than the one we live in now would be a very different sort of place. **A planet no human has ever yet experienced.**

To improve our chances of survival, we need to slow the rate of climate change to give us more time to adapt, and stop the planet warming up any more than is now inevitable.

That means cutting greenhouse-gas emissions drastically as soon – as close to NOW – as we can, to keep levels from going above 450ppm and to start the long process of returning them to 350ppm.

On a personal level, this means reducing your greenhouse-gas emissions from a column you can hold on your outstretched arms to one you could balance on the palm of your hand.

AND HERE IS THE SOLUTION?

STOP.

Just **stop**.

Turn out the lights, close down the power stations, leave the cars at the side of the road, shut down the factories, ground all the aeroplanes.

Our slogan could be "Back to the Stone Age"!

Simple, eh?

NO, HERE IS THE SOLUTION:

Trouble is, this "Back to the Stone Age" approach wouldn't work, even if everyone agreed to follow it, because we can't support 9 billion people (which is how many of us there'll be by 2050) on Stone Age farming and technology.

There are a lot of things we **will** have to stop doing, like driving everywhere, flying every time we go on holiday, eating whatever we like, and having lots of deep, hot baths. But then most of the people in the world have never been able to do those things anyway, so it's only fair that we should stop being so greedy and selfish with the planet's resources.

So "stopping" is part of the solution – but we can't stop growing food, building homes, keeping them warm and light and getting from place to place. At the moment, doing all those things depends on fossil fuels. Not only in the obvious ways, like cars running on petrol, and power stations burning coal or gas. The wheat in your breakfast cereal and the cotton in your jeans needed petrol-powered machines to grow and harvest them, and planes and trucks to take them to the shop you bought them from; the concrete used to build your house was made in a kiln heated by burning coal; and your iPod, your computer and your phone were made from oil-based chemicals in factories powered by fossil fuels.

So we have to change how we do things, which means the solution isn't simple and it isn't just one thing. But it isn't just a dream either. It's being built, right now, from lots of smaller solutions, by people all around the world – solutions that help us cut our greenhouse-gas emissions and solutions that help us prepare for the climate change we can't avoid.

This section of the book is about some of those solutions and the people who are working them out. Some are finding ways to fight climate change through trying to change how we live our everyday lives; others are fighting on a bigger scale, through trying to change what governments and countries do. Reading about them you'll learn more about what a far-reaching problem climate change is – and also that there are as many ways of fighting it as there are people in the world.

Changing Minds

The biggest obstacle to beating climate change is inside people's heads. If you haven't got the message that climate change is real and we need to stop it, then you won't change the way you live or ask your government to help cut greenhouse-gas emissions. As the great scientist Albert Einstein said, "You cannot solve a problem with the same thinking that caused the problem."

Casper Ter Kuile and Emma Biermann are co-founders of the environmental network UK Youth Climate Coalition (UK YCC, ukycc.wordpress.com), which brings together youth organizations for a strong political voice on climate change. They want to make sure that the message gets to as many young people as possible.

"We are the generation who will have to live with climate change and pay for it," says Casper. **"So let's get fired up about it."**

But how do you get people who are pretty occupied with clubbing, drinking and checking out their mates on Facebook to care about the planet?

"You've got to bring climate

Casper and Emma with a polar bear (look carefully!)

All photos: UK YCC

change into people's world, get their heroes to lead them. If the coolest guy in class starts to care about climate change, then others will follow."

The way that climate change is often represented in the media is definitely not the way to do it:

"Telling someone the world is going to end and they are a bad person because they don't switch the lights off is not effective," says Casper. "It just doesn't work to make people feel guilty and powerless."

The message that UK YCC wants to convey is much more positive:

"The things we need to do to tackle this problem will actually give us all a much more enjoyable lifestyle," says Emma.

"Yes," agrees Casper. "Fewer cars, locally-grown food, cleaner energy, better public transport. We'll be healthier and happier and – oh yeah – we'll be fighting climate change!"

from left: Emma, Lauren, from the Australian Youth Climate Coalition, and Casper.

UK YCC encourages members to get active – to tell politicians, local councils, school governors what needs to be done.

"We know there are lots of young people who care about the planet, quietly, at home in their rooms," says Emma. **"YCC will give them the little push they need to get them out of their bedrooms to take some action."**

As experienced campaigners, Casper and Emma know how powerful young people can be as a force for change, not just in their own homes and schools, but on the big political stage too. Casper says:

"A group of 14-year-olds making a well-informed appeal to their MP can have much more effect than adults doing the same."

UK YCC representatives will be at all future rounds of international negotiations on climate change, along with other young climate campaigners from around the world, demanding that governments take action to safeguard their future.

"It's up to us to tell all the delegates that our generation will not accept failure," says Casper.

UK YCC has serious work to do, but having a good time is also an essential

© Greg Armfield / WWF-UK

Casper on the sofa with Minister for the Environment Hilary Benn.

Check out
www.youtube.com/
watch?v=6I0vY6g3iJ0
for more about
the Green Finger Project

Young climate campaigners from all over the world.

component of climate campaigning:

"The more campaigning I do," says Casper, **"the more fun I have."**

And if you don't believe him, take a look at "the Green Finger Project" (see link above). I won't tell you any more about it, but it's a great way to a have laugh with your mates ... oh yeah, and deliver a very important message.

EMMA'S TOP TIPS FOR THE RELUCTANT CAMPAIGNER OR "HOW TO GET OFF YOUR BED AND CHANGE THE WORLD"

Casper and Emma when they started the UK Youth Climate Coalition.

<u>BE A SPONGE</u>: read, watch, listen — soak up anything that makes you angry, passionate and fired up for action.

<u>DO WHAT YOU ARE GOOD AT</u>: whether that's art, theatre, music, talking, listening, writing — your skills will make your campaigning AWESOME!

<u>STEAL IDEAS</u>: you don't always have to come up with your own ideas — it's fine to use someone else's.

<u>REMEMBER — SMALL IS POWERFUL</u>: just as Anita Roddick said, "If you think you're too small to have an impact, try going to bed with a mosquito."

<u>HAVE A GOOD TIME</u>: you'll get through to people better if you work with friends and enjoy your campaigning.

<u>ALWAYS CARRY CHOCOLATE BISCUITS</u>: essential equipment for attracting instant support and boosting campaigner morale!

caspersarcticvoyage.wordpress.com/2008/06/29/ the-uk-youth-climate-coalition

www.ourclimate.ca

www.takingitglobal.org/resources/orgs/ view html?OrgID=34923

www.youthclimatecoalition. blogspot.com

OTHER NETWORKS AND ORGANIZATIONS THAT HELP CHANGE MINDS

Richard Ford – Footprint Friends

FOOTPRINT FRIENDS
www.footprintfriends.com
This is a site exclusively for young people (aged 11–18) to air their views on climate change and enter competitions to win funds for eco-projects. Upload your "footprints" – paint your feet to symbolize the footprint you want to leave on the planet.

C-CHANGE
Young people educating other young people about climate change.

www.switchonswitchoff.org

BEN AND JERRY'S CLIMATE CHANGE COLLEGE
www.climatechangecollege.org/home.php

Runs expeditions to the Arctic with the WWFN, for young people; see their blogs and videos here, plus excellent information on how to change minds and run campaigns.

JULIE'S BICYCLE
Devoted to taking the heat out of music – reducing the carbon footprint of the music biz, including going to festivals.

www.juliesbicycle.com

<u>OTHER</u> WAYS OF CHANGING MINDS

<u>ARTS v. GLOBAL WARMING</u>

TIPPING POINT www.tippingpoint.org.uk

Aims to bring artists and scientists together to help get the message across through pictures, sculpture, books, plays, music and dance.

CAPE FAREWELL www.capefarewell.com

Combines art, science and education to communicate about climate change in new ways. Leads expeditions to the Arctic with artists and scientists and has led two expeditions with young people. Check out expedition blogs, photos and videos.

FORKBEARD FANTASY combine film, performance and animation in a whirl of mayhem. Their show "Invisible Bonfires" is a mad comic parody of climate-change lectures and conferences.

www.forkbeardfantasy.co.uk
www.youtube.com/forkbeardfantasy

Forkbeard Fantasy

"THE 11TH HOUR" is a documentary movie about what we need to do to save the planet, narrated by Leonardo DiCaprio.

Andy Hollingworth

DEMONSTRATIONS

Want to go camping with lots of new friends and make your views on climate change known? Pick up your tent and go on a climate camp, like the one that happened at the site of the proposed new coal-fired power station at Kingsnorth, Kent, in August 2008. For news of the next one go to:

www.climatecamp.org.uk

BOOKS

Kate Evans's cartoon book "Funny Weather" will make you laugh out loud while you learn lots of stuff about climate change (you can look at the whole thing online too).

www.funnyweather.org

Comedian Mark Watson's book "Crap at the Environment" aims to make readers less rubbish at being green.

www.myspace.com/crapattheenvironment

Marcus Brigstocke

POST CARDS

TO SAVE THE PLANET
good50x70.org/2008/gallery/gallery02/

COMEDY

Comedian Marcus Brigstocke went to the Arctic, with Cape Farewell, to see the big melt for himself and bring back jokes. "The Arctic is melting faster than the Wicked Witch of the West in an outdoor bath with the shower on in the rain…"
www.marcusbrigstocke.com/ blog.php

MUSIC/ VIDEO /ART/ INTERNET/ FASHION

The 2008 winners of the DEFRA Climate Change Champions award used all of these media to get the climate-change message across. Look at the stuff they did at **yoursay.footprintfriends. com/content/DEFRAprofiles. aspx** and while you're there look at the rest of the website.

Bad Habits

Humans are good at habits, like always getting a lift to school, or always standing under the shower for half an hour, or always using a hair-drier. But changing old, energy-guzzling habits and developing new CO_2-cutting ones is easier than it seems – especially if there's an immediate reward.

Neil Jennings was doing a PhD at the University of East Anglia when he started noticing that students in the halls of residence were in the habit of leaving the lights on all night. There was no incentive for anyone to bother to switch them off, because students paid a flat rate for their rooms, with no separate bill for electricity.

Neil's thesis was about one of the possible disastrous consequences of climate change – the failure of the Gulf Stream:

Neil Jennings of STUDENT SWITCH OFF, an energy-saving

"If the Gulf Stream shut down now we would have a climate similar to that of Iceland, with sea ice off the south coast and snow on the ground until March every year – it would basically completely mess up our transport system and agriculture."

Neil Jennings

competition between university halls of residence.

Luckily, most climate models predict that this is pretty unlikely to happen – maybe a 5% chance in the next 100 years.

"But," says Neil, **"would you stay on a plane that had a 5% chance of crashing?"**

It's not surprising that Neil's mind kept wandering to all that CO_2 being added to the atmosphere, increasing the risks of nasty climate-change-consequences, just 'cos no one could get into the habit of switching off the lights.

So he came up with Student Switch Off (SSO) – an energy-saving competition between university halls of residence; they would compete against one another to reduce their energy use, and the ones that did the best would get prizes.

"The uni were very keen as soon as I told them about the idea," says Neil, **"as long as I did all the work!"** And there was quite a lot of work to do. First, Neil had to sort out practical details, like electricity meters: for the competition to be workable, the electricity used by each hall of residence had to be separately measured.

Next, Neil needed prizes, good enough to make winning worth while. Luckily he got off to a flying start: **"My first sponsor — Ben and Jerry's — said 'yes' within three hours of my first email! Once I had one on board, the others were more interested."**

Neil ended up with five different companies sponsoring the scheme, providing prizes from free ice cream to cinema tickets and solar-powered iPod gizmos.

The scheme was launched in September 2006, and the students seemed to like the *idea*, but Neil didn't know if they would really take *action*.

"The first indication we had that it was a success was in November, when the meter-readings came in for October and showed a big reduction in energy use."

In its first year at UEA, Student Switch Off reduced the university halls of residence's carbon emissions by 92 tonnes, or 10%. Not huge, but a really significant start, and one that the university liked a lot, as it saved them money. It also got Neil selected by Ben and Jerry's as a "Climate Change Ambassador" to go the Arctic with the WWFN to see the very sharp end of global warming.

"I was already convinced about climate change, but it was still quite shocking to see the changes in the depth of the ice. We drilled cores through the ice showing it was 1.5m thick, where twenty years ago it had been 2.5m."

Neil's Arctic adventures inspired him to roll out SSO to even more universities. In 2007–8 the seven SSO universities on board reduced energy usage by an average of 8.7% and saved a total of over 500 tonnes of CO_2. Four more universities have signed up for 2008–9, and another sixteen are waiting to start in 2009–10.

Odeon Cinemas, one of the sponsors of SSO, have been so impressed that they've started their own "switch off", turning off lights and air-conditioning in their cinemas overnight, saving £15,000 on fuel bills in just six months, and significantly reducing carbon emissions.

"I wouldn't call myself a deep green," Neil says; **"I'm very pragmatic. Whatever takes the most CO_2 out of the atmosphere is best."**

Check out
studentswitchoff.co.uk

LITTLE CHANGES — BIG EFFECT

GLOBAL ACTION PLAN

www.globalactionplan.org.uk/aboutus.aspx

is all about practical changes that everyone can make. It's worked with 300 schools in the UK to reduce their energy use by 11%, and the rubbish they produce by 40% — all by doing small, simple things.

FOOTPRINT FRIENDS' "WOW" OR "WIPE OUT WASTE" CAMPAIGN

provides special monitors that measure just how much energy a home is using, and how much it costs. It makes the link between what you do and the energy you use really clear, helping to change

BAD ENERGY HABITS.

(There are lots of other WOW campaigns around the world, focused on other sorts of waste, like rubbish.)

LITTLE DEMONSTRATORS — BIG EFFECTS

In August 2008 a replica of a coal-fired power station at Legoland was attacked by 2cm-tall Lego demonstrators, who unveiled a banner saying STOP CLIMATE CHANGE. Meanwhile, at the site of the real power station at Kingsnorth, hundreds of real humans demonstrated too.

www.nonewcoal.org.uk/?q=node/24

World Development Movement / Peter Taylor

JUNEAU, ALASKA

THE CITY lost most of its power supply in early 2008 when a series of avalanches destroyed power lines. So citizens just switched off anything that wasn't really needed – half-empty freezers, TVs on standby, lights in hallways. In two weeks they'd cut their use of electricity by 30% – just by remembering to flick a switch or two.

Alaska Electric Light & Power Company

medway says no to dirty power

Keeping Switched On

Most of the electricity in the world at the moment is made by burning fossil fuels – like coal, oil and gas. Which means that every time you switch something on – a computer, a TV, a light – you're putting greenhouse gases – mostly CO_2 – into the atmosphere, into your personal CO_2 column.

Of course, you can cut your CO_2 column by using *less* electricity, but it's hard to use *no* electricity, unless you want to turn off every electrical appliance in your house and sit in the dark, without even a charged-up iPod to keep you company.

So we need new ways of making electricity – and Concentrating Solar Power (CSP) could be one of them. Barrister Polly Higgins was looking for ways to help the planet when she heard about it:

"I got such a buzz as soon as I heard about how CSP worked," she says. **"I knew at once that this was huge, important – a really big solution to the energy problem."**

In fact Polly got such a buzz that she made spreading the word about CSP her new career, switching on politicians around Europe to the potential of this clean energy source. But what is CSP?

"I always ask people if they've ever burnt their hand – or even

fried an ant – using the sun and a magnifying glass," Polly tells me. "Well, if you can fry an ant by focusing the sun through a little bit of glass, just imagine the power of hundreds and hundreds of huge mirrors all concentrating the sun's heat."

Ian Lawrie

Barrister Polly Higgins

So CSP is very big-scale ant-frying – hundreds of mirrors reflect the sun's heat, concentrating it into a super-hot beam. That big heat is used to boil liquid, which drives turbines, changing heat energy into electricity.

"CSP isn't wacky new technology," Polly explains. "The first plants were built in America 25 years ago. So we know it works."

But how do you get electricity after sunset?

"CSP works using heat, and you can store heat in the day and use it to generate electricity after dark."

Of course CSP works best where it's very hot and very sunny – in a desert, in fact, and deserts are not something the world is short of.

"We'd need to cover just 0.3% of the area of the Sahara with

CSP plants to generate all the electricity that Europe, the Middle East and North Africa need."

But isn't it an awfully long way from the middle of the desert to where people live? Polly's got that one covered too:

"Some 90% of the world's population live within 2,700km of a desert," she says.

The idea is that high-voltage cables would carry the electricity into major cities, where it would plug in to the existing grid and be transformed into the sort of electricity used in homes.

It all sounds so perfect that it's hard to understand why the desert isn't already covered in mirrors, supplying electricity from Marrakesh to Moscow, Tel Aviv to Telford. The problem is that plugging new sources of energy like CSP in to an old European electricity-grid system is almost impossible. Every country has its own grid – all different and some very old-fashioned – and a whole lot of energy-generating companies want to keep control of the energy supply, so as to make money. It's a terrible tangle, and it could have blocked the development of new clean energy sources for decades.

Luckily, thanks to the hard work of people like Polly and her colleagues, the European Parliament in Brussels has realized that we really need these new sources of electricity very badly, so they have ordered that all the grids must be modernized and the companies must co-operate so that the electricity systems of every European country are compatible with one another. The target is to complete this work by 2016, so that new, green sources of energy, like CSP, will be able to plug in anywhere and flow all over Europe. By 2020 many homes in Europe could be using electricity generated by a CSP plant in the Sahara! What's more, as the two things many poorer countries have are sunshine and desert, CSP could one day supply clean, CO_2-free electricity to countries where turning on the lights has been a luxury few people could enjoy.

Polly is full of enthusiasm for the potential of CSP:

"It's so exciting to be working with something that's a big solution!" she says; but she's also a realist, and she knows that by 2050 with a world population of 9 billion we'd need 10,000 CSP plants to supply just half the world's electricity if we carry on using and wasting it the way we do now.

"Renewables are only part of the solution," says Polly. **"What we need is a seismic shift in humanity's attitude, so we start to care for our planet."**

Wind, solar, **wave** and HYDRO are renewable sources of energy, so called because unlike coal, oil, gas and the uranium that's needed for nuclear power, they don't run out. They create energy without burning anything – so no CO_2.

Some countries already get some of their power from renewables. Germany, for example, gets 15% of its electricity from conventional solar power – produced by the sort of solar panels you can have on your roof, which generate electricity or heat water. Many people in the UK now have solar panels on their roofs heating water for baths, showers and washing. The Chinese are keen on this technology too and plan to triple their use of solar-heated water in the next few years.

In the UK the government has promised that 10% of our electricity will come from renewables by 2010. The European Parliament has pledged "20, 20, 20 by 2020" – a 20% cut in emissions, and 20% increases in fuel efficiency and the use of renewables.

RENEWABLE DRAWBACKS

The problem with renewables is that they don't supply energy all the time the way fossil-fuel generation or nuclear power does, so the energy they provide needs to be stored for night-time or calm days. At the moment, the technology for storing electricity doesn't work very well – but people are trying to find ways to improve it all the time.

One way to help with the stop/start nature of electricity generated from renewables is to get power from a mixture of different sources, so the chances are at least one of them will be working at any one time ... although when everyone switches on the kettle at the end of *Dr Who* there could be problems.

There are concerns about the effect that wave farms and wind turbines will have on wildlife and on the natural beauty of wild places. Also, wind turbines sometimes use up land that we may need for growing food in the future. So we need to think very carefully about where we put our new, clean energy-making kits.

OFF THE GRID?

All those pylons that stride over the UK countryside are part of the national grid, a single, giant electricity circuit that keeps everyone supplied. The trouble is that parts of it are very old indeed – more than seventy years – and the whole thing is a bit old-fashioned. To make the most of renewables we need a modernized grid and, perhaps, lots of smaller circuits, supplying communities with energy generated close to where people live and work. We could also use new Combined Heat and Power (CHP) central heating boilers in people's houses and offices to generate electricity as well as heat; these should be available in the next five years.

Dale Vince, high-profile eco-warrior and head of Ecotricity, a renewable-energy company, says we can help now by choosing who we get our power from: "You can fight climate change with your electricity bill. Use your need for electricity to bring about new clean sources of it – sustainable ones."

GO NUCLEAR

One simple solution would be to replace our coal- and oil-fired power stations with nuclear power stations. These don't burn fossil fuels, and we'd need only a few of them to meet our needs. France gets most of its electricity from nuclear power (quite a lot of that comes over the Channel to us). The new nuclear power stations have a good safety record and can be built in about five years, so we could all do the same. But over their lifetime nuclear power stations have a big carbon footprint – the uranium they run on has to be mined and transported and the very long-lived toxic waste they generate has to be disposed of. Some people (for example, James Lovelock) think that this isn't a big problem and that we must "go nuclear" to combat climate change and keep the lights on. Other people (like me) would rather live with some power cuts to avoid nuclear.

A nuclear power station in Pennsylvania.

CARBON CAPTURE

China and India can't switch to renewables quickly enough to power their fast-growing industries and cities. So they (and other countries with big coal reserves) are going to be using coal-fired electricity power stations for many years to come. To stop this pouring CO_2 into the atmosphere, we need carbon capture – this is the technology that catches CO_2 and stores it safely, usually underground. Carbon capture isn't quite up to the job yet, but experts say that it will be by 2015–2020, so countries (like the UK) that could manage without coal-fired power stations should do so, until carbon capture is working perfectly (which means a big NO to the coal-fired power station at Kingsnorth in Kent).

Sir Robert Watson, Chief Scientific Adviser to the UK government, says, **"If there's one technology the world has to have, it's carbon capture."**

For **MORE** on our energy options

Take a look at the Energy Saving Trust:
www.energysavingtrust.org.uk/generate_your_own_energy/how_renewable_energy_works

GREEN ENERGY SUPPLIERS

ECOTRICITY

Supplies energy mainly from renewables combined with some from non-renewable sources (in other words ordinary, CO_2-generating ones) to 106,000 homes. Invests lots of money (£250 per customer per year) in building new wind turbines. Dale Vince, their CEO, says, "I run a business to bring change to the world. My interest is the next industrial revolution – how to live without burning up the planet." **www.ecotricity.co.uk**

GOOD ENERGY

Supplies energy 100% derived from renewable sources, mostly wind, with some small-scale hydro and a tiny bit of solar. Good at supporting individuals to generate their own electricity. Juliet Davenport, their founder and CEO, says, "By supplying information about climate change, and showing how we can stop it, Good Energy empowers people to become part of the solution." **www.goodenergy.co.uk**

Driving Mad

Cars that run on petrol produce a lot of CO_2 – 170 kilos per car for every 100km it drives. When you add all the fossil fuels that get burned to make the car in the first place, the greenhouse-gas cloud above each car is even bigger. And there are almost 30 million of them in the UK alone.

Almost half of all car journeys are so short that most people could easliy walk or cycle instead, and some of the shortest of all regular daily car journeys are made by parents taking their children to school.

The solution here is pretty obvious, isn't it? Just get on your bike – and it's Holly Bruford's job to help school students in London to do just that.

"I have the best job in the whole of London," says Holly. **"I get paid to ride around on my bike every day!"**

Holly Bruford works for Sustrans (www.sustrans.org.uk), a UK charity that encourages planet-friendly, healthy ways of travelling. She helps to run a project called Bike It in schools across London.

Bike It aims to get children biking to school instead of getting a lift in a car.

Each school-run car trip produces, on average,

Holly Bruford, Bike It officer

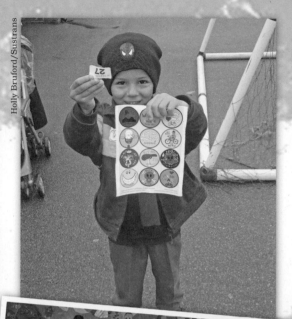

nearly a kilo of CO_2. With hundreds of thousands of children travelling to school by car, that's a lot of CO_2 that could be saved by "biking it". Holly's job is to show children and schools that cycling to school is safe, fun, healthy and good for the environment.

"As a field officer I make my own schedule," she says. **"I might be running cycling-skills workshops for a bunch of children at a school, or talking to the staff about CO_2 emissions. I could be sorting out how to get a cycle shed built or organizing a bike festival to get people enthusiastic about biking."**

Holly's commitment to doing something practical to combat climate change began when she was working for an aid organization in Guatemala:

"In Britain the signs of global

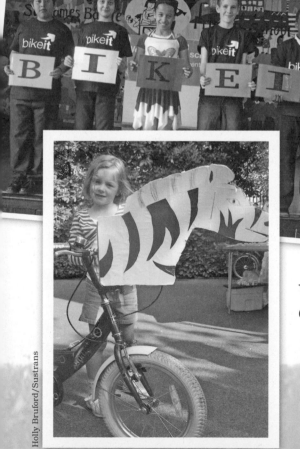

warming are still quite small, but in Guatemala they're huge. It's already changing people's lives and making them much harder. Winters there have become so wet that it's impossible for poor farmers to get their produce to market. So they have no income unless they can find a way to store their crops until spring. In a community on the poverty line, that creates real hardship."

Just before Holly left Guatemala in 2005, a fierce tropical storm caused catastrophic mudslides across the mountain region where she worked. The next-door village was simply wiped out:

"It was just a mass grave. Everyone was killed, because of climate change – caused by things happening in a world those people didn't even known about … our world, my world, back home."

When Holly returned to Britain she was determined to make a difference:

"One of the best things about this job is that I'm working with people with the same morals, and with energy to put into something they really care about. And the kids are great fun!"

Holly and her colleagues at Sustrans are starting to have a real effect. Since the start of the Bike It project, four times more children from the schools taking part are regularly cycling to school, and every year there are more and more schools that want to get involved. But convincing students and schools that biking it is a good idea isn't always easy:

"People often think it'll take ages. One little girl I met got to school at half-past seven because she'd allowed herself two hours to cycle a couple of miles!"

There are real practical problems to be overcome too, but these are just what Bike It was set up to overcome:

"Sometimes," says Holly, "I feel like a fairy godmother. Teachers say, 'Oh, but we haven't got a bike shed,' and I say, 'Here's a bike shed!' Kids say, 'But we haven't got any lights,' and I say, 'Here are your lights!' I'm the 'yes' girl. I'm the girl who says, 'I'll fix that; I'll make that happen.'"

I feel like a fairy godmother

Holly Bruford/Sustrans

Holly Bruford/Sustrans

PLANET-LOVING WAYS OF GETTING AROUND

A

Bikes and **feet** are the best options – but you can't cycle to see your gran 200 miles away, or walk 20 miles to the shops. So the next best option is the **bus** or the **train**. That way you'll be adding nine times (bus) or seven times (train) less CO_2 to your greenhouse-gas column than you would have done going in the car.

Lorries

Almost all the stuff we buy is taken to the shops in diesel-powered lorries. Putting it all on trains instead would release 90% (!!) less CO_2 than lorry transport.

We could also move freight around on canal boats, or even by sailing boat – as some companies are already doing:

www.guardian.co.uk/environment/2008/feb/24/food.carbonemissions

Electric cars

Garages that sell petrol could sell electricity from renewable sources to charge up electric cars instead. It's all possible, but the car companies are not too keen to make the big switch yet, so it may take a few more years. Also, electric cars still take energy to produce, so whatever way you look at it, we're going to need to do a LOT less car-driving. If you've been

VERY BUSY ROAD

really looking forward to driving fast cars, take a look at www.youtube.com/watch?v=oz4mGpwJlSM to see an electric car, but for petrol heads.

Biofuels

Grow a plant, and it soaks up CO_2. Make it into biodiesel or ethanol and run your car on it, and it releases that CO_2 again; overall, the atmosphere hasn't gained, or lost, CO_2: that's the bright idea of biofuels. But most biofuels are a very bad idea, because forests that soak up masses of CO_2, and food crops that people need to eat, are being destroyed to grow plants for making biofuel. You could feed a person for a whole year on the grain it takes to make enough biofuel to fill up one tank, of one car, once. The only "good" biofuel is the stuff that can be made from recycled cooking oil – fry your chips, then fuel your car! For a good example of this, look at what Filipe Alves has been doing:

www.climatechangecollege.org/theaction/ambassadors08/filipemiguelmoreiraalves

For more about
Bad Biofuel Bonkersness:
www.rspb.org.uk/news/details.asp?id=tcm:9-191597

Plane Foolish

I wish I could tell you that planes don't emit any greenhouse gases, that they are as planet-friendly as a field of cute little daisies in the sun. Then we could go on crossing the Atlantic in four hours and going half-way round the world for a weekend.

But they *do* emit greenhouse gases. Lots and lots. In fact, planes are about as planet-friendly as the meteorite in the movie *Armageddon*. It's not that planes are especially inefficient: they produce about as much CO_2 per passenger per mile as a car with four people in it. The difference is that you don't drive to New York. One flight across the Atlantic emits as much CO_2 as a family car does in a year. What's more, that CO_2, plus a cocktail of other greenhouse gases, is emitted high up, where the plane flies, exactly where those gases can do the most damage, causing nearly three times more greenhouse warming than emissions lower down.

So it's clear we *should* be doing much less flying. But what we *are* doing is more and more. By 2030, the UK government says, air travel will have doubled and will be our biggest national emitter of greenhouse gases.

Sadly, Bruce Willis isn't available to blast the plane problem the way he did the meteorite, but we do have Justin Schlossberg and his company noflights. com, instead.

Noflights.com is devoted to making rail and ship transport available and affordable to more people. Justin says:

"We're 100% confident that people on all our trips and itineraries are making a meaningful reduction in their CO_2 emissions."

By booking places on trains, ferries and cargo ships, noflights.com can get you anywhere in the world without a plane.

Hell is for Heroes

Justin, in his band.

Justin knows about no-flight travel because he spent six years schlepping round the planet on a tour bus, as singer with the band Hell Is for Heroes:

"Touring taught me that not flying isn't a compromise or a sacrifice," says Justin. **"It's lots of fun and a great experience. We tell our customers that although, without flights, they may have time to go only half the distance, they will see twice as much of the world."**

At the moment, this kind of travel comes at a price:

"An overnight train from Paris to Rome," Justin tells me, **"costs more than the flight. But again you have to factor in the experience – European overnight trains are really lovely, like nice hotels."**

This is the future of travel, because planes won't work on electricity, like cars, and the extra plants we'd need to grow to make the right sort of biofuels to run planes on could take up as much space as the area of China, which wouldn't leave much room for food or forests. As only a tiny percentage of the world's population can afford to fly anyway, this would seem rash.

Justin has big ambitions for his company:

"My aim is to provide this service for people who want to travel from anywhere to anywhere."

It's clear "noflights" doesn't mean "notravel", but it does mean that if we want to travel a long way, it's going to take days – even weeks – not hours. We need to think differently about travelling: instead of the journey being something unpleasant that you endure to get where you're going, it could become as important as the destination. As Justin says:

"Your journey is part of your holiday."

LOOK — No Wings

Campaign against air travel: PLANE STUPID

is a network of groups taking inventive direct action against airport expansion and aviation's climate impact.

"Bringing the aviation industry back down to Earth."

www.planestupid.com

NOFLIGHTS.com
Noflights will get you there without a plane.

Carbon-offsetting

You'll find a carbon-offset option on most websites where you can book flights. The idea is that you pay someone to plant trees, buy a bit of forest, or give some low-carbon technology to a developing country. This is supposed to soak up the CO_2 your flight emits, so you can fly guilt-free.

There are a lot of problems with this idea, not least that there isn't room in the world to plant enough trees to "offset" everyone's flights. Even if all of the southern hemisphere ran on solar power, we'd still fry if the rest of us went on burning fossil fuels. If we really want to slow climate change we should be reducing air travel A LOT, cutting our emissions in every way we can AND planting trees and helping other countries to use low-carbon technology.

To see how carbon-offsetting is not as good as it seems look at **www.cheatneutral.com** (you will laugh a lot).

To find out how forest-saving can REALLY help see **www.worldlandtrust.org** and **www.carbonbalanced.org**

and **coolearth.org**

THE MAN IN SEAT 61

www.seat61.com

Ex-railwayman Mark Smith began seat61.com as a hobby in 2001, and now it's a full-time job. The site provides free information on travelling by train or ship instead of flying.

LOW-CARBON ADVENTURERS

Ed Gillespie travelled round the world in 2006 without taking a single flight. He says, "In an age when any idiot can get on a plane and twang themselves to the other side of the planet, there is something uniquely satisfying about a long voyage by sea." Read his blog: **www.lowcarbontravel.com/2008/01/freight-way-to-travel.html**

Ryan Van Duzer, broadcaster, travel writer and video film-maker, known as the "Out There Guy" in his native Colorado, USA, proves that you can have great globetrotting adventures with nothing more than a bike and a tent. "Bicycling is the ultimate way to travel and see the world. I get to hear, smell, touch and feel every inch of my adventures." **www.duzertv.com**

Your own adventures without flights

You can cross oceans and continents by train and boat. High-speed trains can get you to your destination as fast as a plane, if you add in the time you spend queuing at the airport.

Ferry boats can do short sea crossings but for crossing the ocean you need a cargo ship. Their CO_2 emissions aren't low, but they are doing an essential job and you can just piggyback as a passenger. But beware of cruise ships! They are so luxurious that they have a carbon footprint three times greater than a plane per person per mile and thirty times more than a train journey!

Rock-Star Food

Next time you go to the supermarket, just take a minute to read the labels on the food. If it says the "country of origin" is Peru, Guatemala, Kenya, Israel, New Zealand, Egypt or somewhere equally far away, it's clear that your dinner is better travelled than you are. It has zoomed around the world like a rock star, burning up aviation fuel and loading the atmosphere with ever more CO_2. And all of that's before you add in the emissions from the tractors, fertilizers and pesticides it took to grow the food in the first place. Even supermarket foods that aren't flown in from other countries do a stupid amount of travelling, from farms to packaging plants, to warehouses, to shops.

And the energy craziness doesn't stop when the food arrives at the supermarket: it's displayed in chilled cabinets, with no doors, next to heaters and bright lights; then people drive their cars to buy it and take it home. If you wanted to design a way of feeding people that wasted the most energy and created the greatest greenhouse-gas emissions possible, this would probably be it.

Duncan Gibson, boss of the organic-food delivery service Abel and Cole, isn't impressed:

Duncan Gibson, MD of Abel and Cole, which promotes food with a low carbon footprint.

www.abelandcole.co.uk

"If you showed a freshly-landed Martian the way we produce and sell food, they'd think it was utterly ridiculous," he says.

So how did it get this bad?

"For the last 30 years," Duncan explains, **"supermarkets have been working out how to sell a lot of food and to sell it very cheaply. So they grow food on a huge scale and everything is centralized."**

That means fewer, bigger farms, and food travelling long distances.

For example, a major UK supermarket is about to build a big meat-processing and packaging plant in Uruguay, to supply UK shops. (Yes, that's Uruguay in South America, and the UK in Europe.)

Duncan comes from a farming family and could see what supermarket-style food was doing to farmers, food and the planet. So he tried to change the supermarkets from the inside, running the fresh-produce side of several major UK companies. But he soon realized he wasn't going to be successful, so he moved to Abel and Cole, who were already supplying organic food that hadn't been on a world tour before arriving on the table:

"About 75% of all the food we supply to our customers is grown in the UK. We do buy in some things from other countries — such as bananas and wine — but we never use air freight. It all comes on boats."

Abel and Cole don't package things the way supermarkets do, either. Almost everything comes in simple cardboard boxes, which customers return, so they can be reused and then recycled when they finally wear out. Everything they sell is organically grown, which cuts down on emissions from chemical fertilizers and pesticides, and finally it's delivered to its customers, so there's no need for energy-wasting freezer units and over-lit, overheated shops.

"Each of our vans delivers to 80 or 90 homes," says Duncan. **"So that's 80 or 90 cars that aren't driving to the supermarket a couple of times a week. But,** he adds, **"we do have trouble with our fuel. We've tried using recycled chip fat (see** *Planet-Loving Ways of Getting Around,* **page 116), but our vans stop and start so much their engines keep blowing up! I'd really love to find a way to sort that out."**

More and more people are shifting away from supermarket food, so companies like Abel and Cole are growing, and working with more and more farmers, bakers and cheesemakers to supply people with food that comes from near where they live. But sometimes food-miles are unavoidable:

"Certain foods grow best in certain areas," Duncan explains. **"We try to use local soils and climate sympathetically, but that means you have to move stuff around."**

Apples, for instance, don't grow so well in the north of England, so Abel and Cole are encouraging farmers in Kent, in the far south-east corner, to replant apple orchards that were pulled up because UK supermarkets started buying their apples from abroad. Duncan's apples will have to travel, but not on a plane from the other side of the world.

Locally-produced food is often cheaper than the imported alternative, but organic foods are generally more expensive because organic farming can't produce such high yields. Duncan hopes that even in a recession, when people have to cut back on their spending, his customers will stick to their decision to buy more planet-friendly food:

"The last thing we should do is pile back into producing food that uses more and more oil. In the long term, fuel prices and the environmental costs will mean most food will be produced and delivered our way."

YUM, YUM, YUM! NOSH WITH A LITTLE FOOTPRINT

Tips on what to eat...

* EAT FOODS IN SEASON. Fresh strawberries in January come from a LONG way away (unless you live in Australia), or were grown in heated greenhouses.

* EAT LESS MEAT AND DAIRY. A kilo of beef is responsible for more greenhouse-gas emissions than three hours' driving AND leaving all the lights on back home. Farm animals produce lots of methane and eat food that could feed humans.

* DRINK TAP WATER. Bottled water is transported a long way, and the plastic bottles take energy to make and most get thrown away. The bottled-water industry in the UK causes 30,100 tonnes of CO_2 emissions a year. For more on bad bottled water, look at www.guardian.co.uk/environment/2008/feb/10/water.foodanddrink

and where to buy food...

* BUY LOCAL. Use farmers' markets (which mostly sell stuff that's produced within 30 miles) or veg-box schemes (which deliver a box of veg and fruit, often organic and mostly local) whenever you can. If you have to choose between something grown locally and in season and something grown organically in another country, choose local.

In the US, look here for help:
www.nrdc.org/health/foodmiles?gclid=CNfvmfeWl5UCFQ2L1QodBDr5fQ
In the UK, type "veg box" or "farmer's market", plus your town
or county, into Google.

* IN THE SUPERMARKET... Read the labels and buy food produced
in your country or state. Ask the supermarket manager to
stock locally-grown food.

Grow your own

*YOU CAN GROW SOME FOOD — even if it's only a pot of herbs
— even if all you have is a windowsill. There are loads of
books, websites and magazines that will tell you how to get
started.

* ENCOURAGE YOUR SCHOOL TO START A VEG GARDEN. For information
on how to get started, look at the Royal Horticultural
Society's Campaign for School Gardening
www.rhs.org.uk/schoolgardening/default.aspa
and **www.teachernet.gov.uk/GrowingSchools/**
or (for your younger siblings) **www.edibleplaygrounds.co.uk**

* HOME-GROWN FUTURE. The droughts, floods and extra-hot
summers that climate change is going to bring are going
to have a big effect on how much food we can grow, and
where. Some countries may no longer be able to grow enough
food to sell to other nations, so it's important that we
try to grow as much food close to home as we can.

Homes for Climate Heroes

Most buildings are as leaky as a sieve. When it's cold the heat leaks out, and when it's hot it leaks right back in again. To keep the temperature inside comfortable, we have to use central heating and air-conditioning a lot of the time. Architect Jim Logan knows that this is more than crazy and expensive; it's quite simply costing the Earth.

"Every dollar you spend on your power bill," he says, **"impacts not only on your finances but on the future of the planet."**

And the impact buildings have doesn't stop there. There's all the embodied energy too – that's the power used to build them: to make the concrete, the steel, the bricks and the glass; to transport all these and put them all together.

"Buildings in the US are responsible for 35% of the country's carbon emissions, and it's growing," says Jim. **"As architects, we have great potential to reverse this trend. We need to invest talent and money now towards the evolution of an architecture that does not destroy us."**

Reversing that trend is what Jim Logan has been doing for more than 30 years. He designs buildings that don't have such a big impact on the planet.

He has perfected the techniques of green design, using super-insulated walls and roofs, double- or triple-glazed windows with special high-tech coatings, orientated to catch heat when it's needed and be shaded when it's not, and skylights to make the best use of natural light. The buildings Jim designs are not leaky at all, in fact they leak so little that they don't need any source of heating or cooling and stay a steady 21°C or so winter and summer, even when the outside temperature drops to −5°C or soars to 40°C. Wherever possible they are made with locally-sourced materials, that are easy to maintain and will last, which all helps to keep embodied energy low.

Why aren't all buildings like this?

"It's cheaper to build things badly than to build them well," says Jim. **"And the average American moves every three years, so if you tell them insulation will pay for itself in five years, they say, 'I won't be here.'"**

But things are changing. Sweden and Norway don't allow badly-built houses – by law their houses must be properly insulated, so they use just a quarter of the energy for heating that US and UK houses do. In his home town of Boulder, Colorado,

Michael Shopenn

Eco-architect Jim Logan

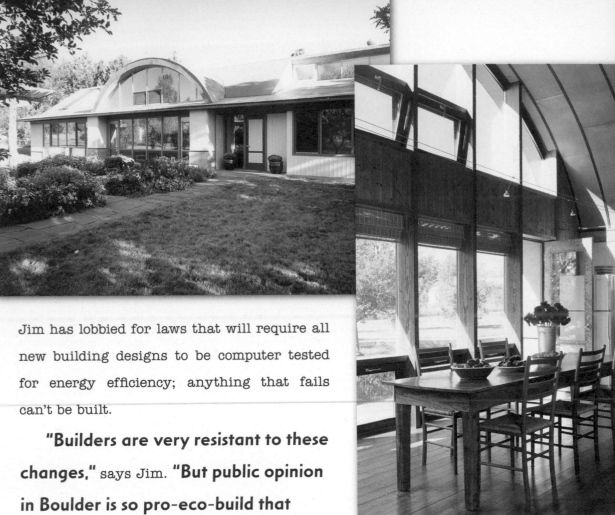

Jim has lobbied for laws that will require all new building designs to be computer tested for energy efficiency; anything that fails can't be built.

"Builders are very resistant to these changes," says Jim. **"But public opinion in Boulder is so pro-eco-build that their opposition has been swept away. They don't even turn up to meetings to oppose decisions any more."**

Jim knows that not everyone can live in a new house, so his latest and biggest idea is the Boulder Energy Project:

"It's simple, but giant," Jim says. **"We're going to look at all the residential buildings in our town and look at their CO_2 emissions**

— all 330,000 tonnes of them — and figure out a cost-effective way to fix them and try to make them all carbon neutral by 2030."

Jim and his team will use every green building trick they know to plug the energy leaks of Boulder's buildings — from the latest in solar power and insulation to putting a fan in the front door to track down draughty holes and then blocking them up with spray foam!

"We're trying to show that it's possible. It's a giant research project, really, and it's generating quite a buzz," says Jim. **"Every architect wants to say they're green now."**

All architectural images: Emily Minton-Redfield EMR Photography

GREEN HOUSE LIVING

CONCRETE PROBLEMS:

To make concrete, you need to heat crushed rock to 1,500°C, which can be done only by burning gas, and creating loads of CO_2. But a new process adds a magic ingredient, so the concrete needs cooking at only 500°C – and you can get 500°C from a giant electric oven, so concrete could now be made using renewable energy.

GOOD IDEAS:

Design makes a difference

The emissions from whole cities can be shrunk if they're designed and planned so that people don't have to drive everywhere, and can walk or cycle wherever they need to go.

"If we have giant cities all over the world, with big highways for big cars, the world is not going to be a sustainable place." Enrique Penalosa, former Mayor of Bogotá

City trees cast cooling shade and provide shelter from cold winds – reducing the need for air-conditioning and heating. And they soak up CO_2!

Architecture to green the desert

Climate change will reduce rainfall and create deserts in many areas, so architects Michael Pawlyn and Charlie Paton have come up with the Sahara Forest Project. They've created greenhouses that produce their own fresh water from seawater using solar power. This will allow almost any food crop to be grown in the middle of even the hottest desert.

GOOD STUFF TO DO AT HOME:

✓ track down draughts and block them up

✓ check your loft insulation ... you need 25cm at least

✓ use windows, not air-con, for cooling

✓ draw curtains as soon as it gets dark to stop heat leaks

SOME GOOD EXAMPLES

Honingham earth-sheltered social housing scheme

Honingham, Norfolk

No conventional heating or cooling system, zero carbon emissions and it stays at 22°C throughout the winter.

BowZed, Bow, east London

Solar panels, a wind turbine and no fossil fuels required.

For more advice check out www.GreenDIY.ie

This website is put together by student Cara Augustenborg to help people make their homes climate-friendly. Cara also put together a little show house at a Dublin shopping centre to show people all the things they can do to shrink their home's carbon footprint.

Maxwell's Photography

Cara, centre, gets ready for some Green DIY.

Dressing for the Climate

I have to start this section with a confession: I am a clothes addict. My T-shirts alone fill two drawers, my double wardrobe bulges and I'm too embarrassed to tell you how many pairs of shoes I have. Every single item of clothing that I own has its own fat footprint, its own little column of CO_2 and trail of polluting chemicals. The cotton in my jeans and T-shirts was grown using pesticides that take a lot of energy to make, and then pollute land and water when they're used. I try to buy things made of organic cotton now, but that isn't exactly innocent either – it takes just as many petrol-powered farm vehicles to cultivate and harvest organic cotton, and it gets transported to the UK on a plane or a huge ship, just like the non-organic stuff. My favourite black trousers are made from polyester, a kind of plastic derived from oil, and my favourite purple sweater is made of wool from New Zealand.

I'm not the only one with this planet-bashing addiction to new clothes: in the last decade the number of items of clothing bought by an average UK girl has gone up from 19 a year to 34! It's clear our clothes habit is costing the planet way too much – but fashion designer Nin Castle could be our salvation:

Nin Castle in her studio.

"The fashion industry is sooo negative!" she says. **"The whole thing — from the way cotton's produced to how it's harvested and made into clothes. I set up my company, Goodone, to try to do something about all that."**

Nin's plan was to design clothes that made people feel good, but didn't have a horrible environmental impact. She began by using organic cotton:

"But it was too expensive and I didn't have any money," Nin laughs. **"So I tried using recycled clothes. I found I could make pattern pieces that would fit onto an old T-shirt or a jersey. I thought, 'Hey, this is just fabric!'"**

Nin had to mix and match material from several different old T-shirts or jerseys to make up one of her designs. But this meant she could incorporate bold contrasts of colours and shapes. The clothes were a big hit, and Nin's business was born:

Danny Rodgers

"My labour costs are high, but my fabrics cost virtually nothing."

Nin is making use of some of the 1 million tonnes of clothing and fabric that end up in landfill sites in the UK every year. She and her team sort through 200 tonnes of old clothes every week, looking for stuff that they can reuse. This simple operation of making new clothes out of old can have a big impact: clothes made in this way have around half the carbon footprint of clothes made from new textiles; if everyone in the UK, every year, bought one item made from recycled fabric instead of new, it would cut CO_2 emissions by the equivalent of 4,500 days' worth of an average household's electricity.

Goodone is still a small company, but Nin wants to have a big effect:

"I want to be on the high street, where I can have the biggest impact and make the biggest change," she says.

So her next step will be to work with big sports-clothing brands, using up their faulty stock and ends of lines, to make her own new designer clothes.

"I want to show the big companies how easy it is to do

Jess Bonham

this. Every high-street shop should have clothes made of recycled fabric."

Nin still loves fashion, even though she wants to change the way it works:

"You've got to be in it to win it," she says. "A lot of ethical design is a bit tame. I don't want to be pious or worthy, I just want to design beautiful, sexy clothes."

Nin's "mix and match" style!

NIN'S TIPS FOR CLOTHES ADDICTS

1. BREAK THE FAST-FASHION HABIT

"Buy ONE thing that you really love and that's really well made instead of three things that won't last."

2. USE A NEEDLE!

"Learn some basic sewing so you can extend the life of your clothes. My favourite jeans started life as wide-legged; now they're narrow-legged, high-waisted trousers."

4. SPEAK UP

"If you don't like what a retailer does – using child labour or non-organic cotton or whatever – write and tell them. You are the customer and they need you."

3. BUY THE GOOD STUFF WHENEVER YOU CAN

"Make SOME of the clothes you buy organic, ethical and recycled even if ALL of them can't be that way. It'll help businesses like Goodone to grow."

1. Washing away the planet

Washing a T-shirt at 60°C, tumble drying and ironing it will generate 4kg of CO_2 in its lifetime. Wash it at 30°C, dry it on a line or an indoor clothes rack and don't iron it, and the CO_2 emissions drop to 2kg.

2. Planet colour

White clothes get dirty more quickly and need more washing to get them clean. Wear colours and patterns that don't show the dirt.

3. Overalls and aprons are planet-friendly

Washing machines, tumble driers and irons use electricity and generate CO_2, so the less you wash your clothes the better. This doesn't mean you have to go around with egg stains on your shirt ... use aprons, overalls and napkins whenever you're doing something messy.

4. Clothes care

Clothes last longer when they are put away (no, this is not just a nasty rumour spread by parents who want you to tidy your room). Also, do not put your clothes in the laundry basket just because you can't be bothered to put them in a cupboard or drawer.

5. Swishing

A swishing party simply means one where you swap clothes. Everyone brings along at least one nice piece of clothing they don't want any more. Then everyone swaps – and goes home with a new wardrobe! You can organize your own swishing party.

Keeping Gaia Green

These green areas of tropical forest are one of Gaia's most important temperature-regulators.

One of the most important parts of Gaia's temperature-regulation system is the green girdle of tropical forests around the Earth's middle. This soaks up CO_2 and releases life-giving oxygen, as trees grow; it breathes out water vapour-making clouds and rain which cool the hot, sun-soaked tropics. And of course it holds on to a lot of CO_2, keeping it locked up in the chemicals that make roots and trunks, leaves and branches.

It doesn't take a genius to see that, in our current climate crisis, tropical forests could be a big, big help, and we *should* be protecting every single tree.

Roberto Pedraza

" **I support the notion that tropical forests and other critically threatened habitats and their wildlife must be saved at all cost.** "

SIR DAVID ATTENBOROUGH

(Sir David is a natural-history expert, wildlife film-maker and author. Several generations of people have been turned on to wildlife through his programmes. He is my **TOTAL** hero.)

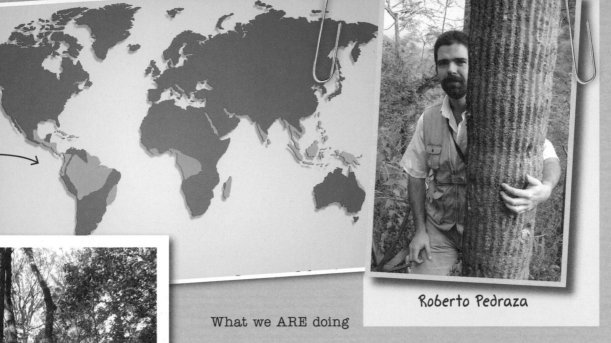

Roberto Pedraza

What we ARE doing is cutting trees down as if our lives depended on it. Around fifty football pitches worth are cleared every year for timber, or to make room for farming, or, craziest of all, to grow biofuels for cars. This deforestation releases the CO_2 stored in the trees, it stops those trees soaking up more CO_2 and it releases another powerful greenhouse gas, nitrous oxide, from the exposed soil. Deforestation creates more greenhouse-gas emissions than all the cars, planes and ships in the world. One-fifth of all the CO_2 released each year comes from deforestation. Not only that, but it plugs into a feedback loop – fewer trees means less rain, and less rain means fewer trees.

While governments argue about how to safeguard tropical forests, hard-working individuals all over the world are down in the woods, trying to save trees. Roberto Pedraza is one of them.

Roberto lives in the Sierra Gorda, a beautiful mountainous area of Mexico.

Roberto lives in the Sierra Gorda, a beautiful mountainous area of Mexico, about ten times the size of the Isle of Wight with many different kinds of natural tropical forest. Roberto works for Grupa Ecologico Sierra Gorda (GESG), a conservation organization founded by his parents:

"They were deeply concerned by the loss of the forests," Roberto explains. **"People were cutting down trees for fuel, for timber and to make space for farming."**

The loss of the forests was starting to make life harder for the residents of the Sierra Gorda: without trees to soak up rain, and roots holding the earth, soil began to wash away, and floods and landslides were a problem.

"My parents began to work with their neighbours, educating them and planting trees."

A deforested slope before soil-conservation works began. Before slopes can be replanted, walls are built to hold soil in place.

All Roberto Pedraza

Roberto's parents' hard work paid off: the Sierra Gorda is now a reserve protected by the Mexican government and receives money from conservation organizations across the world. But local people are still the cornerstone of its success.

"Local people are our biggest allies," says Roberto. **"Around 34,000 participate each year in tree-planting, fire-fighting and conservation activities."**

Roberto works with local landowners to encourage them to keep existing forests and to plant new native trees where forest has been cleared. The benefits for Sierra residents have been huge – water supplies are safer, soil erosion has

Ancient trees like those in the Sierra Gorda forest lock away many tons of CO_2 in their trunks, roots and branches.

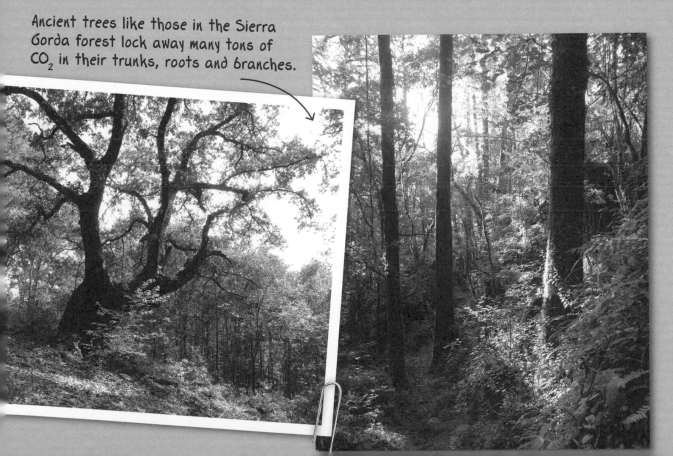

been cut, and there are more local jobs in forestry and eco-tourism.

"After nineteen years," says Roberto, **"they are convinced of the benefits of conservation."**

Through protecting their forests, Roberto and the people of the Sierra Gorda are helping the whole world to fight climate change now and in the future: now, by not cutting down fully-grown forests and so keeping CO_2 safely locked up in trees; and in the future, by planting trees that will soak up lots of CO_2 when they get big in twenty years' time.

"We made an inventory of the carbon stored in our ecosytems and found that 124,065,851 tonnes of carbon is stored in the forests of the Sierra Gorda! So by protecting them, we avoid all that carbon being put into the atmosphere."

The forests of the Sierra Gorda are a lot more than a "carbon store". They hold 327 different species of birds, 131

There are lots of reptiles and amphibians in Roberto's forests, like this baby salamander.

species of mammals and an astonishing 2,300 species of plant. As climate change could make 30% of the species alive today extinct, the Sierra Gorda is fighting not only the causes of climate change, but the EFFECTS too, by keeping its species safe.

"Carbon is a great tool for conservation. We have returned 13,000 hectares of deforested land back to forest, and reduced fragmentation of forests," says Roberto. **"This means more and better habitats for wildlife."**

The Sierra Gorda's rich store of carbon and species means companies in the US and Europe are keen to pay GESG to preserve their forests – and keep CO_2 locked up – to "offset" their own CO_2 emissions. Some climate-change campaigners are dead against carbon-offsetting (see *Plane Foolish*, page 118, and cheatneutral.com), and it's true that if businesses and countries see it as an excuse not to cut their CO_2 emissions, it won't help at all in the long run. But if companies pay to save forests AND cut emissions, it could be a powerful way to lock up CO_2 and save species from extinction.

Right now, companies and individuals buying carbon offsets help to pay for GESG's work, allowing Roberto to safeguard more and more forest.

"Without our forests we are doomed," he says. **"We need to protect what's left and recover what has been lost. Deforestation is not just CO_2 released, it means a loss of biodiversity; forests should be protected jewels."**

WOODLAND WAYS — keeping woods woody

... IN THE TROPICS

A big part of deforestation is driven by international business — logging, mining and farming, especially for biofuels. The good part of this is that big international companies have to listen to public opinion — if their customers don't want them to cut down rainforest, then they have to stop.

CAMPAIGNING ORGANIZATIONS

Greenpeace

Well-respected, expert campaigners on every part of the environment. To find out how to help with rainforests:

www.greenpeace.org/international/campaigns/forests
www.greenpeace.org/international/photosvideos/photos/nomadic-penan-leader-along-seg#

The Rainforest Foundation

Check out their Tree-man blog. A man dressed as a tree travels around London to spread the word about forests and climate change:

www.rainforestfoundationuk.org/Tree-man?offset=6

A barren slope before reforestation.

... AND WOODS AT HOME

Forests in the cooler parts of the world don't have such a huge role to play in the control of climate change, but they can still help to keep CO_2 locked up and protect biodiversity.

USEFUL ORGANIZATIONS

The Woodland Trust

www.woodland-trust.org.uk/
campaigns/index.htm

Runs tree-planting days — you can go along as a volunteer and give some practical help to the fight against climate change.

BACKYARD WOODS

Plant a tree in your garden or somebody else's garden. Persuade your school to create a mini-woodland in the school grounds. Trees don't lock up much CO_2 when they are young, but in 20 years' time, when they are growing fast, they can lock CO_2 away in their woody trunks and branches. A single tree at maximum growth takes 7.5–13kg of CO_2 out of the atmosphere each year. Every little helps.

Roberto Pedraza

WOODS UNDER WATER

Sea problems: acid and warm

The b-zillions of tiny floating sea plants — the phytoplankton — lock away as much CO_2 as all the world's land plants. But climate change is making the seas warmer and more acid, so phytoplankton may not grow so well and may soak up less CO_2, plugging us into another feedback loop — more global warming means less phytoplankton means more global warming.

Sea problems: coral reefs

Coral reefs are often called the rainforests of the sea. They hold close to a million species of animals and plants. Corals like warm water, but if it's *too* warm, they die, and more acidic sea makes it harder for corals to grow. So climate change could wipe out almost half of the world's reefs.

Liz Wood/Marine Conservation Society

Clownfish among the tentacles of an anemone.

Green turtles,
beautiful but threatened
marine reptiles.

Peter Richardson/Marine Conservation Society

Sea solutions

Slowing climate change will help plankton and reefs, but we can take the pressure off them in other ways, such as by cutting pollution and preventing reefs from being used as building materials.

For more sea solutions:

The Marine Conservation Society (MCS) **www.mcsuk.org** and **www.mcsuk.org/coolseas** You can help survey and clean-up beaches with the Marine Conservation Society, on Beachwatch/International Coastal Clean-up Weekend every September.

The World Wide Fund for Nature (WWF) has loads of ocean conservation projects **www.panda.org/about_ wwf/what_we_do/marine/ problems/climate_change/**

> **There is strong evidence of the rich countries causing the problem and poor countries being adversely affected, and thus it is time for the rich countries to address their obligations to reduce climate change...**

MARY ROBINSON

(barrister, ex-President of Ireland, and UN High Commissioner for Human Rights 1997–2002 — and she's telling it like it is: "It's our fault, so we need to put it right").

Martin Wagner and his son Jasper.

Martha Belcher

Lawyers for the Earth

If someone dumps rubbish in your garden, they're breaking the law and they must pay you for the damage they've done to your property. But no one owns the atmosphere, so when someone dumps greenhouse gases in it, how can they be made responsible for the damage that causes?

Lawyers like Martin Wagner of the environmental-law firm Earthjustice (whose motto is "...because the Earth needs a good lawyer") are working out how this can be done.

Martin is using human-rights laws – some of the most important international laws there are – to help peoples like the Inuit to take action on climate change. Human-rights laws protect basic human needs, like a place to live, food and safety, and the culture that helps define who you are, and many people around the world are already losing their homes, their livelihoods, their safety and their culture because of climate change.

"One of the strengths of the law," Martin says, **"is that it's a way to tell stories in places where they can make a difference. Human rights are about stories**

All photos taken by Martin Wagner

we can all relate to; stories about things we all
need; powerful stories that can motivate powerful
people to take action."

Back in 2001, Martin was one of the first lawyers to
see the link between climate change and human rights:

**"The Inuit were beginning to think about how
to raise their plight with the world,"** Martin tells me,
**"at the same time as I was starting to think about
using human rights to address climate change."**

Martin sees the effects of climate change in the place closest to his heart, the
Sierra Nevada Mountains, where snowpack is decreasing and plant and animal species
are threatened with extinction due to warming temperatures.

Martin began working with the Inuit Circumpolar Council on the effects that climate change was having on the lives of the Inuit. He and his colleagues interviewed Elders across Canada and in Alaska:

"It was remarkable to me how clearly they saw the effects of climate change on their environment," Martin says. He found that the Inuit's detailed knowledge of seasonal changes, particularly relating to ice, was passed down the generations and clearly showed how much the Arctic climate was changing.

"Ice is their highway, their grocery store, their shelter, even," says Martin, **"and all those things are being destroyed by global warming."**

It was clear to Martin that climate change was taking away the Inuit's human rights, and that the country with the biggest greenhouse-gas emissions – the United States – was clearly most responsible for that. So Martin and his team of lawyers helped the Inuit leaders and Elders to present a petition to the Inter-American Commission on Human Rights in Washington, the capital of the US. Martin said at the time:

"The United States makes up only five per cent of the world's population, but emits one-quarter of global-warming pollution. This petition calls on the United States to respect its human-rights obligations and take effective action to immediately reduce its contribution to the Inuit's injuries."

Before 2005, when the Inuit's petition was finally presented, talk of climate change was mostly technical and dry, but the petition changed all that. It made big news and helped people really understand the serious effects of climate change on humans.

"There is no international police force to enforce human-rights law," Martin explains, **"but discussing climate change in this way is**

very important because it influences decision-makers and nations and helps motivate ordinary people to take action."

The commission has not yet decided what to do about climate change and how it affects Inuit rights; but as a result of the Inuit's petition – and similar actions – the United Nations is now studying the link between global warming and human rights. Martin and his team have given the Office of the UN High Commissioner for Human Rights a legal document explaining how climate change violates people's rights and asking the UN to take action to help.

Martin is convinced that human-rights law is a powerful tool to use in the fight against climate change.

"Human rights crosses boundaries between liberals and conservatives. It puts governments under pressure by making them ashamed of what they've done wrong, but also making them aspire to do better!"

All over the world people are starting to tell the stories of how climate change is affecting their lives through human-rights law, helped by lawyers like Martin:

"We are all in this struggle together," he says, "and each of us is essential to making the world a better place."

Rights AND Fights

RIGHTS AT RISK FROM CLIMATE CHANGE

TUVALU

Tuvalu is a tiny country just 26 sq km spread over 9 islands in the middle of the Pacific. In 40 years it will be under the sea, and its 11,000 inhabitants will need some other country to give them a home. Tuvalu's neighbour, New Zealand, will accept only 75 Tuvaluan refugees per year, which would mean the last islander would reach safety 106 years after Tuvalu had drowned.

At the moment the UN doesn't recognize "country under water owing to climate change" as a good enough reason for someone to be an official refugee with a right to settle somewhere drier. But the Alliance of Small Island States, which represents other low-lying island countries such as the Maldives and Fiji, is working with lawyers to change things. (And to help publicize the fate of Tuvalu, Japanese photographer Shuuichi Endou is photographing every single one of Tuvalu's 11,000 people!)

CARTERET ISLANDS
Papua New Guinea

These tiny tropical islands will be under the sea even sooner than Tuvalu – by 2015, in fact.

The islanders will have to go to the bigger island of Bougainville to live.

Find out more about the Carteret Islands:
www.youtube.com/ watch?v=fRxpLnfv6xA

BANGLADESH

Bangladesh is the next country in line to have its human rights battered by climate change. Much of it is less than 1m above sea-level. A 40cm flood would affect 94 million people, causing food shortages and outbreaks of water-borne diseases like cholera and dysentery.

FIGHTING WITH THE LAW

THE INUIT VILLAGE of Kivulina in Alaska is being washed away because of eroded sea ice, rising sea-levels and increasing storms. The whole community needs to move to another site, at a cost of some $400 million. So, with the help of lawyer Matt Pawa, Kivulina is suing Exxon Mobil, 8 other oil companies, 14 power companies and a coal company for causing the problem in the first place, and for conspiracy to mislead the public about the science of global warming.

GAIA'S RIGHTS

SUNDAY 28 SEPTEMBER 2008 was a big day for Gaia – for the first time in history it isn't only humans whose rights are protected by law. The people of Ecuador in South America have voted for a new constitution that recognizes that other species and wild places have the right to exist undisturbed and protects that right by law. This is the first big step towards the new and respectful attitude we all need to have towards our planet.

WINNING
WITH THE LAW

SIX GREENPEACE PROTESTERS tried to paint "Gordon Bin It" on the chimney of the proposed new coal-fired power station at Kingsnorth in Kent. They got as far as "Gordon" before having to stop, but still caused £35,000 worth of damage. But when the case came to court in September 2008, the jury ruled that the protesters had a right to cause damage to the chimney to try to prevent the far greater damage that the coal-fired station would cause by contributing to climate change.

Hezel (4th from right) at the climate change conference in Bali.

Baltz Tribunalo, Plan

Listening to Children

Hezel was just 16 when she spoke to United Nations delegates, and journalists, from all over the world at the UN Climate Change Conference in Bali in December 2007. Hezel wrote in her blog at the time:

"I was not so nervous during the press conference ... at last I was able to tell everyone about the situation of children in our communities."

Hezel's community is a village on the island of Masbate in the Philippines. Hezel told the conference how, in her lifetime, climate change has caused the number of typhoons and storms to increase, bringing life-threatening flooding and landslides. She told them how, even when the immediate danger of the storm has passed, children are still affected: "There is failure of crops due to climate change," Hezel wrote in her blog, "and many children are not able to go to school because they have to work because their parents' income is not enough."

Children are much more vulnerable than adults to the disasters that climate change brings: being small makes them more easily overcome by water

FEMA/Leif Skoogfors

Baltz Tribunalo, Plan

Hezel fielding journalists' questions at the Bali climate conference, explaining why children's views about our environment are important.

or mud; when crops fail because of flood or drought, they are the first to die of starvation; they are more easily killed by diseases such as cholera, dysentery and malaria – all of which increase with climate change; and they suffer badly if they are separated from their families and have no one to care for them.

As children are the people worst affected by climate change, it's vital that they have a big say in what's being done about it. The organization Children in a Changing

Floods and typhoons destroy crops, businesses and homes.

FEMA/Andrea Booher

Nick Hall, environment enthusiast.

Climate (CCC) is helping children's voices to be heard in their own communities and in the big wide world. CCC sponsored Hezel and other young delegates to attend the climate-change talks in Bali, and the organization works with children and young people across the globe.

"Children come up with ideas about how to solve problems," says Nick Hall of CCC. **"They have a longer perspective than adults and no prejudices."**

Children are also particularly good at spotting the potential risks from climate-change disasters such as landslides and floods, because when they are outside playing they notice more than adults. Nick runs a scheme called Disaster Risk Reduction, which encourages children to make "risk maps" of their communities to show what the danger points are when disaster strikes:

"Children at a school in El Salvador spotted that a quarry on a riverbank was causing a risk of landslides and floods in their community," Nick tells me. **"They ran a campaign to get the mining stopped. They got their local government to stop the mining along their bit of the river and even over the border in Honduras."**

Campaigns like these change the way children are treated in their communities; grown-ups start listening, which makes children an important force for change. An elder in a village in Sierra Leone summed up what a lot of grown-ups feel: "We are amazed by the capacity of children to understand and explain the range of risks and hazards faced by our community. They wake us all up to reality."

There are now many places in the world where children are helping their communities to prepare for the effects of climate change: planting trees to prevent landslides and provide flood barriers; teaching other children what to do when a typhoon strikes; reducing mosquito-carried diseases by clearing up stagnant water where mozzies breed; and of course speaking out and telling the world their stories, as Hezel did. Following his conversations with Hezel and the other young people, UN General Secretary Ban Ki-moon told the climate-change negotiators in Bali:

"I've spoken to these young people, and it's your job to sort out their future!"

In the nine months following Hezel's return from Bali, the Philippines suffered three typhoons, one cyclone and more floods and landslides.

"We want and have the right to be able to grow up in a sustainable and safe world."

LEON, 16

Leon was a member of Plan UK's Children's Advisory Panel when he said this. Plan UK helps children in poor communities around the world and listens to what children say.

CHILDREN speaking out

Read Hezel's blog
and the blogs of other young
delegates at Bali and more
recent UN climate-change talks:

**childreninachangingclimate.
blogspot.com**

**Young people doing good climate-
change stuff**

**www.childreninachangingclimate.org
/new_ccc_documentary_showing_
how_children_are_prote.html**

Nick and CCC will be helping more young people to
speak on the world stage at future UN meetings on
climate change, working with organizations who
help kids get heard:

African Youth Initiative on Climate Change (AYICC)
"If students don't act against climate change, who will?"

Energy Action Coalition
US campaigning organization started and run by young people

Asian Young Leaders for Climate Forum (AYLCF)
Great video on youtube about the need for someone
to speak up for the 30% of people alive today who will be
affected by climate change but are too young to vote:

www.youtube.com/watch?v=JqesLQ4ZTuE

NASTY numbers that will go UP with climate change

175 million
Number of children likely to be affected by disasters caused by climate change every year from now

3.5 million
Number of children who die every year from malnutrition

AND
800 thousand
Number of African children under 5 who die every year from malaria

350.org
New youth-led global campaign to unite the world around a target atmospheric-greenhouse-gas concentration of 350ppm CO_2. Great animation on **www.youtube.com/watch?v=s5kg1oOq9tY**

Peace Child International (PCI)
Check out the booklet about climate change produced by an international group of young people "Two Degrees of Separation Between Hope and Despair".

2degrees.peacechild.org/?sec=book&site=d1

Big Science

You only have to think of the different locations of a couple of human cities to see that human beings are good at coping with all sorts of climates. In Moscow you could get frostbite on a normal January day, but to cope with a chilly winter afternoon in Sydney, you'd just need a sweater. But if Sydney and Moscow suddenly swapped climates, there would be chaos. This is the big problem that climate change presents: unpredictability. How do you know when to plant your crops if the rainy season doesn't arrive at the time it used to?

This is where the work of the IPCC can help. The Intergovernmental Panel on Climate Change is a collaboration between more than 400 scientists from 120 countries. Its job is to use the best research into the Earth's climate to estimate how it will change in the next 20–100 years, how this might affect people across the world and what humanity can do about it.

Scientist Beth Holland

All four of the IPCC reports have been an important influence on what governments and the UN do about climate change. But the fourth report, published in 2007, was the most important:

"The evidence in the fourth report was more compelling, and more convincing," says Professor Beth Holland of the National Center for Atmospheric Research (NCAR) in the US, one of the lead authors of the last two IPCC reports.

"When I did the distillation of all the scientific research I was awed once again by the strength of the evidence."

The report woke up the whole world, and the world's governments, to the reality of human-made climate change.

But the job of the IPCC isn't simply to say, "Houston, we have a problem." Collaboration between scientists, and between scientists, economists and politicians, is a key part of its work:

"It's really important," Beth tells me, **"that we translate scientific information into the impact it has on economics and on people's lives. We have to make sure that our transfer of scientific knowledge is as good as possible."**

One of the main tools that the IPCC uses to create a big picture of climate change worldwide, and its impacts, is computer modelling. But recently some things in the real world – such as the Arctic ice melt – have been happening faster than the IPCC models predicted. The models also struggle to reflect the seasonal changes in greenhouse gases caused by plant growth and decay. So for the next IPCC report, Beth and her colleagues need to add more detailed information about how climate works now, to make the models better at predicting what will happen in the future.

"We're going back to first principles," say Beth, **"taking a more careful look at the ability of the Earth's natural systems to soak up greenhouse gases, or release them and make matters worse."**

Beth, right, at Bridal Veil Falls, Rocky Mountain National Park.

Kate Lajtha

Much of this huge "soaking up" depends on some of the planet's smallest inhabitants – microbes. This links to the early part of Beth's career, when reading about James Lovelock's Gaia had a big effect on her thinking:

"I realized that there was a bridge between the very small-scale activities of microbes in the soil and in the sea, and the composition of the atmosphere."

This link between the small and the big picture is what the IPCC is good at: linking scientific detail with consequences for millions of people. It's a link that helps to give us back that essential ingredient – predictability.

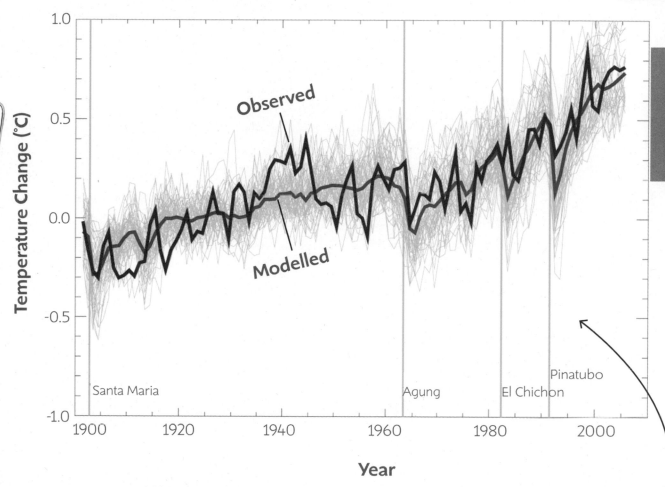

after the IPCC graph in the First Assessment Report of the 2007 study, FAQ 8.1 Figure 1.

This graph shows how the world's temperature REALLY changed between 1900 and 2000 and also how climate models SAY it changed. This is how climate models like the ones Beth works with are checked — by the opposite of forecasting, "backcasting", which means looking at temperatures that have already been measured.

A Short History of

TREATIES AND DEALS

1987 THE MONTREAL PROTOCOL

Scientists say, "...there's a serious hole in the ozone layer and we need to fix it." The UN listens and the Montreal Protocol, an international agreement to cut emissions of hole-making gases, is signed. This leads to the formation of the IPCC.

1988 CREATION OF THE IPCC

1990 FIRST IPCC REPORT

The UN recognizes the need to talk about and act on climate change. From this time information from the IPCC feeds into the world community and gradually starts to spur action.

1992 UNITED NATIONS EARTH SUMMIT IN RIO DE JANEIRO

Countries agree on the United Nations Framework Convention on Climate Change (trips off the tongue, doesn't it?). The UNFCCC doesn't set any targets for cuts in emissions, but agrees that climate change is a problem and that the aim should be to stabilize climate. Not exactly big, but a start.

1995 SECOND IPCC REPORT AND UN MEETING IN BERLIN

Aims to give the UNFCCC some teeth. It is agreed that industrialized countries (who caused climate change in the first place) should be the first to make big cuts in emissions. The US has a tantrum and says it won't cut unless developing countries do too.

So there!

1997 KYOTO PROTOCOL UN MEETING IN KYOTO ON UNFCCC

Sets targets for cuts in emissions of 5.2% of 1990 levels for industrialized countries from 2008 to 2012. Pretty feeble, but a start. The problem is not enough countries sign and ratify (i.e. sign AND then say they'll stick to it) for it to become law.

2001 THIRD IPCC REPORT

Makes even stronger statements about climate change and how humans are probably the cause of it.

2005 KYOTO PROTOCOL

Signed by enough countries to become law. The US is still sulking about how difficult cutting emissions is for America, so doesn't sign. Luckily the American people have more sense, and 600 mayors of US cities have now pledged to keep their cities to Kyoto targets. California now pledges 80% emissions cuts by 2050.

But Kyoto is not completely toothless: it has set up ways in which developed countries can help poorer countries to preserve forests, put in new renewable energy sources and change old polluting industries to cleaner, low-carbon ones. These projects are estimated to be keeping 2 billion tonnes of CO_2 out of the atmosphere.

2005 DECEMBER BIG MEETING OF UN CLIMATE-CHANGE DIPLOMATS

Tries to get agreement on what to do when Kyoto runs out in 2012. US negotiator walks out, and the only agreement other countries make is to talk about it all again.

2007 FOURTH IPCC REPORT

Makes the boldest statement yet about climate change and makes headlines world-wide. There can be no doubt any more: it's happening and we have to do something about it.

2007 UN MEETING ON UNFCCC IN BALI

Serious wrangling to try to agree real action. The European Union pushes for 25–40% cuts by 2020, but China, the US and Japan say "no way". An agreement to make "deep cuts" in emissions, but with no actual figures, is finally reached, but the US has another tantrum and says "no" – and then, at the last minute, says "yes". So in the end there's an agreement with US support, but a pretty weak one.

This is BIG. The time left for the world to slow climate change is running out. Copenhagen is "the now or never moment". Climate campaigners from all over the world will be there to try and push the UN climate negotiators from each country into making an agreement that will really DO something.

Make sure you have your say by joining one of the campaigning organizations or writing to your MP (see *Changing Minds*, page 88).

I don't know what happened in this meeting because at the time of writing it hasn't happened yet.

ALL TALK AND NO ACTION? Not quite: while governments wrangle with one another on the international stage, individual states and businesses are really getting to grips with the fact that "deep cuts" actually MEANS what it says. Remember California's example.

> 66 **Whatever you can dream you can do, begin it. Boldness has genius, power and magic in it. Begin it now.** 99

JOHANN WOLFGANG VON GOETHE

(pronounced Ger-ter)

(Goethe lived in Germany around 200 years ago and was a writer, poet, scientist and philosopher (brainy people back then put their fingers in a lot of pies). It seems to me to be just the sort of thinking we need now: dream it, do it, do it now.)

Seeing the Future

How would you like to cycle to college or to work on tree-covered paths and live in a house where the roof tiles made the electricity for the lights and collected water to run the taps? How would you like to work in an office with flood defences on the ground floor and a wind turbine on the roof? How would you like to live without traffic jams, and travel in high-speed trains? How would you like your town to be such a clean, green, unpolluted place to live that you never thought of going on foreign holidays?

This is the future that Professor Mark Maslin, leading climate scientist at University College London, thinks is possible for humanity:

"This is what the world would look like in 50 years if we shifted to a low-carbon economy."

It sounds wonderful, but how are we going to get to Mark's rosy future? He thinks the best and most effective way is by making the world a FAIRER place.

"There are two major problems facing humanity in the 21st century: global poverty and global warming," says Mark. And he thinks we can tackle them both together.

Poor countries want to improve the lives of their people, to make sure that everyone gets enough to eat, a place to live, education and health care. All that takes energy. If the energy comes from cheap fossil fuels, then however much emissions-cutting the rich countries do, it won't make any difference.

"China is building a new coal-fired power station every four days," says Mark. **"That's going to make global warming worse."**

The alternative is to pay developing countries to use energy sources and other

Mark Maslin

Mark Maslin in the Arctic in 2007, when he took twelve teenagers along to educate them in the science and art of climate change.

technologies with low emissions. This would work through what's called a "cap and trade" system. This means that rich countries would set a limit on the volume of greenhouse gases they were allowed to emit – a "cap". To reach that target they'd have to cut emissions, increase energy efficiency and start to use renewables as a source of energy. But they could also "trade", which means they'd pay a poor country to start using new low-emission technology – and the amount of emissions this would save could add to the rich country's tally of emissions cuts. The "caps" would be set at lower and lower levels, to reduce the rich countries' emissions bit by bit and keep a steady flow of money and clean technology going to poorer countries.

A system like this has been used in the US to make industries cut their emissions of other polluting gases, such as sulphur dioxide. What's more, it was much, much cheaper to do than anyone expected.

"Cap and trade" could mean that everyone wins, Mark says, because:

"Poor countries get richer and rich countries get cleaner!"

As a scientist, Mark sees the solutions very clearly, but he knows that to change things, science must engage with politics and business. He talks to politicians and business people and puts them in touch with other top climate scientists.

"My tightrope walk is between giving people good reliable scientific information and not telling them how to do their job."

The next round of UN climate-change negotiations is happening at the end of 2009. These will decide what the world does about climate change when the present (pretty hopeless) Kyoto agreement runs out in 2012. Mark would like to see a "cap and trade" system that involved the US – the biggest greenhouse-gas emitter now – and India and China – who will be the biggest greenhouse-gas emitters in 30 years' time. Mark would also like to see an agreement to "contract and converge" – which means people in rich countries "contracting" their carbon footprint so that they are nearer to – they "converge" with – the carbon footprint of people in poor countries, so we'd end up with a small carbon footprint for everyone in the world. Mark says:

"In my opinion, global warming is good for humanity; for the first time in humanity's history we have to tackle the unequal distribution of global wealth."

Mark's hopefulness about our future comes from his studies of our past – of human evolution over the last 100,000 years:

"We're the greatest weed the planet has ever produced. We can survive anything!" he jokes.

But of course it would be nice if humans did a bit more than just "survive" and end up chewing on cat bones round a campfire of old sofas. It would be nice to hold on to civilization, and to do that we must have something to aim for:

"If we can have a vision of the future that's worth working for, then we can get there. All the solutions exist and there's no barrier to achieving a very different world from the one we live in now."

FUTURE CITY

Take a look at the plans for the Chinese eco-city Dongtan. It will be built on an island and will be home to half a million people by 2050. All its energy will come from renewables, and its food will be grown on the island to reduce food miles.

www.arup.com/eastasia/project.cfm?pageid=7047

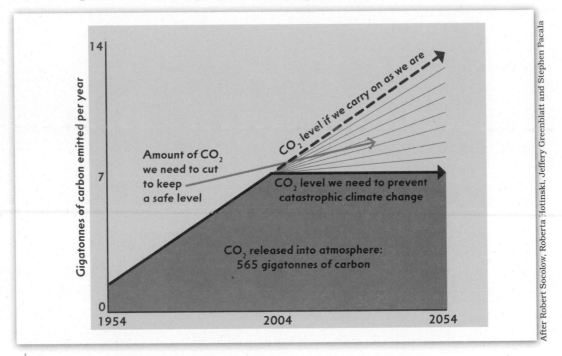

After Robert Socolow, Roberta Hotinski, Jeffery Greenblatt and Stephen Pacala

GET A WEDGIE FOR GAIA!

In spite of the slow progress with international agreements on cutting emissions, many people are waking up to the fact that cuts have got to be DRASTIC. This can seem pretty daunting, but US scientists Stephen Pacala and Robert Socolow of Princeton University have come up with a brilliant idea called wedge theory, which got climate experts, campaigners and politicians very excited.

Just imagine the graph of greenhouse gases in the atmosphere, rising up over time like a steep hill. Now imagine that graph stopped dead, chopped off, with no more rises after this moment. What you're left with is a fat wedge, between where we want emissions to be – not rising – and where they are going right now – up and up. This wedge shows the greenhouse gas we have got to STOP emitting. Stephen and Robert's idea was to break that mega wedge down into seven smaller wedges, and then find ways to get rid of them. It was easy!

There are fifteen different ways to get rid of those seven wedges, right now, using what we already know:

> ❯ Using low-energy light bulbs and other efficient electrical gear in homes and businesses takes care of one whole wedge. One down, six to go...
>
> ❯ Doubling the fuel economy of cars (how many miles they do to the litre), and halving the distance we travel by car, takes care of two wedges.
>
> ❯ Stopping deforestation and doubling our rate of tree-planting – another wedge.

Just three simple things and half the cuts we need are done ... and there are twelve more options on the list for making wedges disappear.

You can even play this as a game. Check out the website:

www.princeton.edu/~cmi/resources/stabwedge.htm

66 **It always seems impossible until it's done.** 99

NELSON MANDELA

(Mandela was the first democratically
elected President of South Africa.
He spent 27 years in prison because
he stuck up for freedom and
equality for all South Africa's people.
So he knows a lot about achieving
impossible things.)

CONCLUSION

When I started writing this book I was pretty gloomy. Climate change **was** big and scary and I **didn't** think I, or anyone else, could make a difference. But I'm not gloomy any more. In fact I'm quite excited because I've started to hear a sound, sometimes like a distant rumble of thunder, sometimes like a raindrop close to my ear. It's the sound of people changing. It's there in all the conversations I had with the people in this book; it's there in all the practical details about insulating houses or designing electric cars; it's there even in all the wrangling of UN climate negotiations. I think there's a shift happening in people's hearts and minds, not just towards the need to save our skins from climate change, but towards a more deeply respectful relationship with the planet that's given us life. It could be the sound of our species, finally, growing up.

Sandy Lovelock

Section Three

Afterword

by James Lovelock

Gaia Warriors is a wonderfully surprising phrase but it is the right title for this book. Some people see Gaia as the mother of everything alive, all-powerful, with a religious significance as part of God's creation; others as the name of a scientific theory about the Earth system. I see her as something that includes both of these ideas, and if we accept that, despite pretending otherwise, humans are war-loving animals, the words "Gaia" and "warriors" do indeed go together.

Warriors do not march to have a friendly discussion, or even an argument. Warriors march to battle and usually intend to win and make sure that their beliefs prevail. Almost all past human history is made up of brief spells of peace interspersed with long periods of war, and whenever war happened and whatever side we were on, we convinced ourselves that we were in the right and that the war was just.

In this, the 21st century, warriors may be faced with an older and simpler form of conflict: that of fighting for survival.

Unconsciously we set in motion the conditions for this war two centuries ago when we began to take more from the Earth than we could ever pay back.

It was not simply by using fossil fuel for energy but also by taking the natural forests and turning them into farmland. These two acts, which made food and medicine abundant, enabled our numbers to grow until we took more from Gaia than she could give. Now we are like the victim of a loan shark, with debts larger than our means to repay them.

Gaia, the Earth system, regulates the planet so it always remains habitable, but to do so she needs the natural forest ecosystems intact. What we humans have done by taking them for ourselves alone is to make the Earth uninhabitable. I think it unlikely that anything we do will alter the course of this change. Nobody – not the cleverest scientist nor even a committee made up of Nobel Prize winners from each of the sciences – can with certainty predict the world of 2030 and tell us how to live peacefully there. Nor can they tell us how to restore the Earth to the lush and habitable state it was in sixty years ago. There are no sure answers, and Gaia, the Earth system, is moving faster than we can respond, still less oppose its motion.

Survival is our only option and, before long, some people will find that their part of the Earth is less harmed by climate change than others. Naturally those whose land becomes desert or is flooded and can no longer provide food and water will move to where there is plenty. Because of our natures, war between these haves and have-nots is inevitable. There will not be food and water enough for both. Sometimes the invaders will win and other times the defenders; what matters is that there are survivors so that there continue to be humans on the Earth. The ultimate survivors will probably include some powerfully effective Gaia warriors, and we will have evolved another step towards a new and perhaps more intelligent species or humans.

What a wicked, wasteful way of progressing, you may think. But war is like this, and never forget that evolution by natural selection is also a blind, cruel process. How else could a feathered monstrosity of the Jurassic evolve into the exquisite perfection of a streamlined swallow? The answer is that countless numbers of less-perfect losers lost in that passage to perfection.

> ## " Nobody ... can with certainty predict the world of 2030 and tell us how to live peacefully there."

To turn the clumsy animals that we are now into streamlined intelligences that can serve as the information system and warriors of our planet will not happen quickly or easily.

Other organisms, more important than we are, started as disastrous mistakes whose unrestrained growth did massive planet-wide damage. Tiny green bacteria heedlessly polluted the air over 2 billion years ago with a poisonous, destructive gas – oxygen. Pollution far more deadly than anything we have done so far. Yet evolution allowed Gaia to adapt and then use oxygen to support life. It took more than a billion years, but from those first polluting bacteria there evolved all planetary life, even giant redwood trees and a world that animals could inhabit.

It has taken Gaia 3.5 billion years, more than a quarter the age of the universe, to evolve humans, a social animal intelligent enough and capable enough to show her how stunningly beautiful she is when seen from space through the eyes of astronauts and when compared with her dead siblings, Mars and Venus. We are a part of Gaia, as are all things alive, whether tigers or slime moulds, and consequently our thoughts are hers. Through us, she begins to understand her history and place in the universe.

Let us look forward to the time when our descendants have evolved to become Gaia's brain – clear in thought and clear in vision – and Gaia's T cells, her warriors, the true defenders serving the first intelligent planet in our galaxy.

MORE GOOD PLACES TO GET INFORMATION

WEBSITES

The Hadley Centre for Climate Change Research
Really good, clear information on the science of climate change:
www.metoffice.gov.uk/research/hadleycentre/

AUSTRALIA AND NEW ZEALAND

Climate Change in Australia
www.climatechangeinaustralia.gov.au

Australian Government, Department of Climate Change
www.climatechange.gov.au

New Zealand's Climate Change Solutions
www.climatechange.govt.nz

Greening Australia/Green Corps
greencorps.greeningaustralia.org.au

BOOKS

Global Warming: A Very Short Introduction by Mark Maslin
Takes you through all the science, the politics and potential solutions to a very positive vision of human future.

The Rough Guide to Climate Change by Robert Henson
Well explained, really clear and nicely written.

(If you read just one book, it should be one of the two above.)

Heat by George Monbiot
Good ways of getting out of the mess we're in.

The Revenge of Gaia by James Lovelock
Really beautifully written explanation of what Gaia is, how she controls our climate and the science of how we've messed it all up.

Funny Weather: Everything You Didn't Want to Know About Climate Change But Probably Should Find Out by Kate Evans
Funny, clear and easy to read (and available online) cartoon guide to the basics.

GLOSSARY

Greenhouse gas
Any gas in the atmosphere that traps heat and prevents it from escaping to space. The gases that make up most of the atmosphere – nitrogen and oxygen – don't do this, but some of the gases that are found at quite low concentrations do have this heat-trapping effect.

Main greenhouse gases:
CO_2 (carbon dioxide): a natural part of the atmosphere, taken up by living plants and breathed out by animals and plants and released from their bodies as they die and decay. Also released when anything burns, so that human burning of fossil fuels – coal, gas and oil – greatly increases the amount of carbon dioxide in the atmosphere, where it stays for 100 years.

CH_4 (methane): has a much more powerful heat-trapping effect than carbon dioxide, but luckily there's much less of it about and it survives just 10 years in the atmosphere. Released from wetlands, rice fields and domestic animals, and could be released from natural stores deep under the oceans if the seas warm too much.

Water vapour: a natural part of the atmosphere as without it clouds couldn't form and rain wouldn't fall. Quite a weak heat-trapper, but still has a big heating effect because there is so much of it – and more and more as the Earth gets warmer.

Ozone: a natural part of the atmosphere, protecting us from harmful parts of the sun's rays. It's also released when sunlight shines on some pollutants. In the wrong place and in the wrong quantities it can interfere with heat loss from the upper atmosphere.

Other greenhouse gases which exist in very small amounts include CFCs (chlorofluorocarbons) and nitrous oxide, both released from industrial processes.

Paleoclimatology is the study of climate in the distant past. Paleoclimatologists look at sediments from ancient lakes, ice cores, tree rings, coral reefs and even ancient tribal records, working like detectives to track down evidence of what Earth's climate and atmosphere were like in the past. Understanding how climate changed in the past helps to predict how man-made climate change will affect the planet in the future.

IPCC (Intergovernmental Panel on Climate Change) is a big co-operative project involving hundreds of top scientists from countries all over the world. They work together to study all the very best research on climate and climate change. They put it all together in very detailed reports that help governments decide what should be done about climate change. Their excellent reports are available to everyone on the internet.

Carbon footprint is a measure of the quantity of greenhouse-gas emissions a person, an organization or even a whole country is causing. This involves adding up the direct emissions – say from your central heating boiler or the car you drive – and the indirect ones, like the emissions that were created by growing the food you eat or by making the products and services you use. It can be a very tricky calculation for big organizations or countries, and even for individuals, but it can help to show what are the best changes to make to reduce emissions most.

Carbon offsetting is the idea that you can cancel out some of your carbon footprint by paying for something to happen that soaks up greenhouse gases – such as planting a tree, saving a bit of rainforest or installing low-energy light bulbs or solar power. It's a good idea but sometimes the companies that offer offsetting are just in it for money and have very little REAL impact on emissions. So choose carefully – or, better still, CUT the size of your footprint AND pay for something that takes some greenhouse gases out of the atmosphere.

Carbon trading is really just offsetting on a big scale – huge companies or even whole countries. The basic idea is that rich countries who produce the most greenhouse gases pay poor countries to keep their footprint small and help them to introduce low-carbon technology instead of the old-fashioned energy-guzzling sort. At its

best it could mean that poor countries get their hands on some of the rich countries' money and get free new clean and green technology. At its worst it could mean keeping poor countries back, and allowing rich countries to go on belching out greenhouse gases like always.

Cap and trade could be a way of making carbon trading work at its best. The idea is that a limit, or cap, is set on the amount of greenhouse gases any country can emit. This limit is lowered year by year so the total amount of greenhouse gases spewed out goes down. To keep within their limit, countries can either just cut their emissions or they can cut and trade emissions with other countries whose carbon footprint is so low they don't even have to cut to meet their limit. But the limits still fall year by year, so all countries end up with a similar, smaller footprint.

Gulf Stream is the commonly used name for part of the Atlantic thermohaline circulation, which is the warm salty current of water that flows up from the South Atlantic, past the west coast of Britain and up to the Arctic, where it cools, sinks and flows south again. It's just part of the giant system of currents that carry warmth of the tropics and cool of the poles around the globe, helping to create familiar patterns of climate. One of the possible outcomes of climate change is the disruption of these currents, such as the failure of the Gulf Stream, which helps to keep Britain mild and wet.

INDEX

ACKNOWLEDGEMENTS

With thanks to Beth Aves,
Genevieve Herr, Neil Jennings.
Sylvia Knight, Sandy Lovelock.
Mark Maslin and Caz Royds.

Also to the organizations
who helped including UK
Youth Climate Coalition, Footprint
Friends, CarbonSense, World
Land Trust, Royal Meteorological
Society and Tipping Point.

The author and publishers wish to thank all those who so generously
gave of their time and supplied photographs and diagrams for this book.
